THE PARADIGM REFERENCE MANUAL

Art Lyons
University of Wisconsin-Eau Claire

Patricia E. Seraydarian
Industry Consultant

Marie Longyear
Consulting Editor

PARADIGM

Developmental Editor . . . . Sonja Brown
Copy Editor . . . . Sylvia Warren
Cover Design . . . . Pollock Design Group
Text Design . . . . Brad Olsen
Composition . . . . Gustafson Graphics

Acknowledgements

Thank you to the following reviewers for their valuable contributions to the development of this reference guide: Dr. Gary McLean, University of Minnesota; Dr. Carol Pemberton, Normandale Community College; and Elsie Larson, University of Maine-Machias.

Business report illustrations in the business documents section adapted from figures in *Keyboarding: A Mastery Approach, Comprehensive, Second Edition*, published by Paradigm Publishing Inc., 1990.

Library of Congress Cataloging-in-Publication Data

Lyons, Art.
   The Paradigm reference manual / Art Lyons, Patricia E.
Seraydarian, Marie Longyear, consulting ed.
     p.   cm.
   Includes index.
   ISBN 1-56118-370-9
   1. English language—Rhetoric—Handbooks, manuals, etc.
2. English language—Usage—Handbooks, manuals, etc.
I. Seraydarian, Patricia E. II. Longyear, Marie. III. Title.
PE1408.l95 1992
808'.042—dc20   92-9243
                                CIP

CONTENTS

TO THE USER

For most people, the purpose of writing is to communicate clear messages that help achieve company or personal goals. Good business writing is not a goal in itself but a skill needed to meet business goals. With this distinction as its guide, *The Paradigm Reference Manual* combines three valuable qualities: it is selective, up to date, and easy to use.

Special Features

This manual focuses on the language and formatting problems that business students and employees are most likely to experience. The suggested solutions are current, realistic, and practical. Just as the rules and guidelines presented are those most relevant to the business setting, the exceptions discussed are those most likely to confuse or frustrate readers, providing a trouble-shooting guide to the most common writing problems.

Because technology has affected writing style and the writing process itself, this manual incorporates hints and shortcuts called TECH TIPS wherever relevant to the topic. The TECH TIPS point out the ways in which computer technology has changed writing standards and the writing process, and they offer strategies for using technology to communicate more productively in writing.

Finally, to accommodate the individual needs of writers, blank pages have been included at the beginning and end of the manual parts. These pages allow you to add notes and reminders about your own special usage problems--those few rules and special word usages that you have trouble remembering. You also may want to attach labeled tabs on pages you refer to repeatedly.

How to Find Answers to Your Questions

The Paradigm Reference Manual provides various means of accessing information quickly and easily:

The detailed *table of contents* and the opening page of each major part offer an overview of each part's contents. Within these parts, sections are clearly labeled to help you scan headings and find needed information.

The detailed *index* in the back of the manual lists topics, often in various ways, to help you find specific topics of interest quickly. In addition, the *Quick Reference to Common Writing Problems* that appears on the inside of the front cover will help you immediately locate answers to the most common writing-related questions.

When you are unsure of which word in a pair of related words to use, look them up in *Part Nine: Word Usage.* This section discusses the most commonly confused and misused words and phrases, providing examples of correct usage. A second part defines common computer terms. Skim both sections to become aware of the words and phrases covered.

Finally, the many *cross references* throughout the manual allow you to move quickly from one section of information to related information located in different sections or parts.

A Final Note

The authors and publisher welcome your comments and suggestions regarding *The Paradigm Reference Manual.* Please forward any comments you have to The Paradigm Reference Manual Editor, Paradigm Publishing Inc., 280 East Case Avenue, St. Paul, MN 55101.

THE WRITING PROCESS

- Define Your Purpose
- Identify Your Reader
- Select Your Information and Plan How To Organize It
- Write Your First Draft Quickly and Plan To Edit
- Make Strong Paragraphs Your Building Blocks
- Use the Active Voice
- Edit and Proofread

PART ONE

NOTES

THE WRITING PROCESS

An effective letter or memo does not simply appear on your paper or computer screen. Instead, it begins to take shape when you think carefully about the situation within which you must write, when you define your purpose for writing. It continues to develop as you consider your reader, the information you must communicate, and the way in which you plan to present that information. Finally, a document that communicates clearly is the result of good writing and good rewriting; you can usually improve anything you have written. This section recommends a process for approaching any writing task.

Define Your Purpose 101

Knowing your purpose for writing is the foundation for any written project. Before you begin writing your memo, letter, or other document, ask yourself the following questions:

What am I trying to accomplish? What is my purpose for writing?

- To inform someone?
- To request information or products?
- To respond to a question or request?
- To persuade someone?
- To direct someone?

Identify Your Reader 102

As you define your purpose, you will need to develop a good picture of the person who will be reading your document. Ask yourself:

Who is my reader? What do I know about my reader that will help determine the best approach?

- Is the audience one person or a group?
- Is my reader a coworker, a subordinate, a superior, or a customer?
- How is the reader likely to feel about my message?

103 | Select Your Information and Plan How To Organize It

Once you have defined your purpose and identified your reader, decide what information you will include. Ask yourself questions such as:

- What does my reader want or need to know?
- What information must I include?
- What information will help my reader respond positively?
- What information should I not include?

To answer these questions, you may find it helpful to spend a few minutes listing all the information you *could* include in your document. You may also find it helpful to write a rough draft of your document. Write the draft quickly, including any information that comes to you. Once you have it all on paper, you can work with it, deciding what to include and what to leave out.

When you have decided what information to include, consider how you will organize that information. Ask yourself:

In what order should I present the information to best accomplish my purpose?

- Most important to least important
- Least important to most important
- Causes leading to some effect
- An effect followed by its causes
- Chronological (first occurrence to last)
- Problem followed by proposed solutions
- Response to several questions in the order in which the questions were asked
- Steps in a process (first step to last)
- Proposal or request followed by reasons

However you organize your ideas, think about your document as having a beginning, a middle, and an end, each with its own purpose. The following is true whether you are writing several paragraphs or a single paragraph:

Beginning
- Introduces main idea or subject
- Gets reader's attention
- Establishes positive tone

Middle
- Contains more detailed information and support for main idea
- Leads reader logically to the conclusion intended by the writer

End
- States writer's conclusion and action reader should take
- Maintains (or reestablishes) positive tone

See section 202, page 14, for information on editing the organization of a document. See section 201, page 13, for guidelines on editing information. See section 1034, page 306, for information on outlining.

> *Tech Tip*
>
> As you ask yourself questions about your topic and audience, quickly list ideas (words and phrases) on your word processor screen. When you cannot list any more, clarify your thinking by combining ideas, by moving subpoints under major points, and by rearranging your list to represent a logical flow of ideas. Print this "outline" and use it to write your first draft.

Write Your First Draft Quickly and Plan To Edit   104

Once you are ready to write, do not allow yourself to stare at a blank sheet of paper (or the computer screen) for more than a few seconds. A first effort is rarely a final draft, even for the best writers; therefore, write something to get yourself started. Let your purpose, reader, and organizational plan guide you, but

Tech Tip: If you find that you're interrupting your keying to edit, try turning down the screen brightness so you cannot see what you are keying until you have finished with that topic. This strategy should allow you to focus more on completing a first draft.

don't let them stifle you. Keep going even if you occasionally lose your focus. Once you have a full draft, you can add or delete information, reorganize, and edit sentences.

105 | Make Strong Paragraphs Your Building Blocks

Most of your written business communication will be too complex to be conveyed in a single sentence. Memos, letters, and even simple informal messages often (though not always) require that you state a general idea and follow with more information about that idea: support for the idea, reasons, examples, explanation, further discussion, and so on.

If you include one main idea in each paragraph, you can move your reader through complicated information idea by idea—paragraph by paragraph—until you believe your reader can draw a logical conclusion.

Occasionally, a good paragraph is a single sentence. More often, a good paragraph is a group of sentences that focus on one main idea. This focus on a single idea is called *unity*. Good paragraphs also help the reader understand relationships between ideas (from paragraph to paragraph) and between ideas and their supporting details. This clarity of relationships is called *coherence*. Both unity and coherence improve when a paragraph begins with a sentence that states or implies the main idea.

Contrast the two paragraphs on the opposite page, both of which are describing the same event.

Version 1

Within minutes after meeting the interviewer, the applicant began to ask interesting and thoughtful questions about the company where she hoped to work. The interviewer talked about the company: its history, its achievements, and its goals for the future. He taught her much about the company's priorities and values. For example, this company was researching ways to recycle its products before most people even knew about recycling. It also won a presidential award for outstanding customer service. She knew a lot about the company, and she got the job.

Version 2

The applicant's job interview went well. Within minutes after meeting the interviewer, she began to ask interesting and thoughtful questions about the company where she hoped to work. Her questions prompted the interviewer to talk about the company: its history, its achievements, its goals for the future, and its priorities and values. By the time the interviewer began asking her questions, she knew a lot about the company. This knowledge helped her answer the interviewer's questions about her potential role in the company, and she got the job.

Version 1 seems to be about an interview, but it lapses into a discussion of the company. It then returns briefly to the interview. The main idea is difficult to identify, and the paragraph lacks coherence. Because it has no clear main idea, it leaves many questions in a reader's mind about how all the details relate to one another.

By contrast, version 2 contains a main idea that is easy to identify: the woman's interview went well. Furthermore, all the details in the paragraph support its main idea; the paragraph has unity. Its coherence is also better than that of the first paragraph. The stated main idea increases the coherence. In addition, the writer repeats phrases to show the reader how the ideas fit together. Notice how the following phrases help to make the paragraph coherent: *Within minutes, Her questions, By the time,* and *This knowledge.*

Remember, good paragraphs:

- Build a clear document
- Focus on a single idea (unity)
- State the main idea as directly as possible
- Support the main idea with any needed details
- Help the reader understand relationships (coherence)

 When you write or edit, you may find it difficult to focus on a specific paragraph because paragraphs before or after distract your attention. Try moving or copying the paragraph to another screen (split screen or second screen). When you have finished writing or editing it, you can move the paragraph back to the original screen.

106 | Use the Active Voice

Use the active voice most of the time. Active-voice sentences use fewer words and are more direct than passive-voice sentences. For example:

$$\overset{\text{s}}{}\quad\overset{\text{v}}{}$$

Passive voice: The policy *memo was written* by your manager.

$$\overset{\text{s}}{}\quad\overset{\text{v}}{}$$

Active voice: Your *manager wrote* the policy memo.

In the active-voice sentence, the subject (*manager*) is the person who performed the action (*wrote*). This structure allows the active-voice sentence to omit two weak words that serve only to lengthen it: *was* and *by*.

Although the active voice is more direct and efficient, the passive voice is useful at times. Use the passive voice when:

- Your writing is so formal or impersonal that you must avoid names and pronouns, as in formal reports
- Active-voice options sound awkward or forced

- You want to improve sentence variety (*see section 203g, page 22*)
- You wish to deemphasize the subject of the sentence

In the following pair of sentences, for example, the passive voice directs attention to the mistake but not to the people making the mistake:

Active	*Passive*
Bruce and Consuelo spent too much on last year's sales meeting.	Too much was spent on last year's sales meeting.

See also section 203h, page 24, for information on editing passive-voice sentences.

Edit and Proofread 107

Editing and proofreading are essential to good writing. Planning and drafting allow you to get your information on paper; editing and proofreading help you communicate your ideas as clearly as possible to a reader.

Part 2 discusses editing and proofreading at length.

NOTES

EDITING AND PROOFREADING

- Edit Information
- Edit Organization
- Edit Sentences
- Proofread Your Document
- Check the Appearance of Your Document
- Proofreaders' Marks

PART TWO

NOTES

EDITING AND PROOFREADING

Editing and proofreading are the final steps in producing a document that communicates effectively. Although the processes are closely related and are sometimes handled simultaneously, there are a few important distinctions to remember. Editing usually involves checking and revising content as well as style. That means checking to see that the document's organization is logical, that sentence meaning is clear, and that the most effective words are used. Editing in this sense is typically handled by the writer. If you are asked to edit another's work, know your limits before you begin. You may not be able to change another person's work as extensively as you would your own because you cannot know the writer's intentions. Also, you must be sensitive to that writer's preferences, particularly if that person is your boss.

Proofreading involves checking a document's mechanics, including errors in punctuation, capitalization, spelling, grammar, and format. Proofreading can also involve comparing a printed document against an edited manuscript, making sure that all indicated changes have been made. Because it is the final stage before a document reaches its audience, proofreading should be as thorough as possible.

This section outlines the steps for editing and proofreading documents.

Edit Information	201

Once you have a full first draft of your document, reconsider your purpose and your reader. Ask questions such as:

- Does your document include all the important information?
- Have you said too much? Can you cut any information?
- Have you said too little? Is there information you can add to improve the communication with your reader?
- Have you used the best words? Are they the right level of formality? Does each word contribute to your meaning?

See section 103, page 4, for guidelines on selecting information.

Once you have all the information you need, consider how you have organized it. Ask yourself questions such as:

- Will your reader be able to identify early in the document your purpose for writing?
- Is the information presented in a logical order?
- Does the order of the information help your reader see connections among your ideas?
- Does the order of the information lead your reader to the conclusion you intend?
- Do you provide a clear and positive conclusion?
- If you want a response, will your reader know exactly what you want?

See section 103, page 4, for information on organizing documents. See section 105, page 6, for information on paragraphs.

Tech Tip

To edit your document for information and organization, you may want to check each main-point statement you make. Scroll through your document and highlight the main-point statement of each paragraph. Copy the statements to another screen, keeping them in their original order. Then read them to make sure you have represented all important points and that those important points appear in a logical order.

203 | Edit Sentences

a. Check That Sentences Are Complete. Be sure to use grammatically complete sentences in your writing, except in the least formal situations. Some sentences that sound like complete sentences, especially when read aloud within a paragraph, may be missing necessary elements; these are sentence *fragments*. Some sentences may be made up of more than one complete sentence connected incorrectly; these are *run-on* sentences.

Sentence Fragments

Wrong: One thing is important. Taking the time to check all your work. [*Taking the time to check your work* is not a sentence. It is a long verb phrase.]

Rewrite: Taking the time to check all your work is important.

Wrong: He will receive benefits. If he can fill out the form correctly. [*If he can fill out the form correctly* is not a sentence. It is a dependent clause.]

Rewrite: If he can fill out the form correctly, he will receive benefits.

Run-On Sentences

Wrong: You will receive a raise in January Raul will be promoted then also. [Two full sentences run together without punctuation.]

Rewrite: You will receive a raise in January. Raul will be promoted then also.

Wrong: Both of you may receive a large bonus in February, neither of you will receive one as big as Steve's. [Two sentences connected incorrectly.]

Rewrite: Both of you may receive a large bonus in February, but neither of you will receive one as big as Steve's.

See also section 418b, page 89, for more information on run-on sentences. See appendix D for more information on clauses, phrases, sentence fragments, run-on sentences, and comma splices.

b. Arrange Sentences To Emphasize the Most Important Ideas. Knowing what you want to emphasize and writing to make your emphasis clear will help you communicate with your reader. Burying an idea within a sentence tends to deemphasize the idea. Often, you can emphasize the main idea of a sentence by placing it at the end of the sentence as in the samples below:

The report on last month's sales contains some bad news.	*Emphasis on* bad news

or

The report that contains the bad news covers last month's sales.	*Emphasis on* last month's sales
There was tension in the conference room.	*Emphasis on* conference room

or

The conference room was filled with tension.	*Emphasis on* tension
The seminar called *Managing Stress* was good.	*Emphasis on* good

or

We attended a good seminar called *Managing Stress.*	*Emphasis on the subject of the seminar:* Managing Stress

c. Place Related Words Together. Edit your sentences so that modifying words, phrases, and clauses are as close as possible to the sentence elements they modify. The placement of the word *only* in the following three sentences shows how word order can change meaning:

Only he may have two days off. [No one else may have the time off.]

He may *only* have two days off. [He gets nothing else, only the time off.]

He may have *only* two days off. [He gets no more than two days off.]

Note how the rewritten sentences below clarify the meaning of the original sentences:

Unclear: Managing the office last week, the problems piled up for him. [*Managing the office last week* appears to modify *problems*.]

Rewrite: Managing the office last week, he saw the problems pile up. [*Managing the office last week* modifies *he*, as it should.]

Unclear: The assistant took his boss to lunch, *who was leaving next week*. [*Who* was leaving next week, the assistant or his boss? The sentence does not make the writer's meaning clear.]

Rewrite: The assistant, *who was leaving next week*, took his boss to lunch. [Modifies *assistant*.]

or

> The assistant took his boss, *who was leaving next week*, out to lunch. [Modifies *boss.*]

Unclear: The new assistant encountered a tired boss, several coworkers' questions, and a dozen roses *on her desk*. [What was really *on her desk?* Does *on her desk* modify *roses* only?]

Rewrite: After encountering a tired boss and several coworkers' questions, the new assistant was pleased to see a dozen roses *on her desk.*

See sections 318–320, pages 55–61, for information on using adjectives and adverbs.

d. Provide Clear References for Pronouns. Check sentences containing pronouns to ensure clear pronoun reference. In some cases, you may have to remove a pronoun and repeat the reference. In other cases, you may have to provide a missing reference or revise the sentence to avoid the problem:

Unclear: Bob and Manuel disagreed about the report. He thought it should be revised. [Who is *he?*]

Rewrite: Bob disagreed with Manuel about the report. Bob thought it should be revised.

or

> Manuel disagreed with Bob, who thought the report should be revised.

Unclear: The manager complained about the lack of motivation and the failure to follow the principles of goal-oriented management, but this has now improved. [What does *this* refer to?]

Rewrite: The manager complained about the lack of motivation and the failure to follow the principles of goal-oriented management, but staff motivation seems to have improved.

See section 313, page 46, for information on pronoun-reference agreement.

e. Express Similar Ideas in Similar Form. When sentence elements are similar in content and function, their form should be similar as well. This concept is called *parallel structure* or *parallelism*:

Not Parallel: Kao was witty, intelligent, and had an outgoing personality.

Rewrite: Kao was witty and intelligent and had an outgoing personality.

Not Parallel: Marta sorted mail, assisted Ms. Wills, and letter filing for Ms. Jervis was one of her jobs.

Rewrite: Marta sorted mail, assisted Ms. Wills, and filed letters for Ms. Jervis.

Not Parallel: We picked up our food in the cafeteria, but lunch was eaten out on the lawn.

Rewrite: We picked up our food in the cafeteria but ate lunch out on the lawn.

Not Parallel: My partner likes the health club and working out in the gym.

Rewrite: My partner likes going to the health club and working out in the gym.

See section 1034d, page 307, for information on parallel structure in outlines.

f. Remove Unnecessary Words. Unnecessary words make your message longer and may make it more difficult to read. As you edit sentences, remove any words you can delete without changing the meaning or making the sentences difficult to understand. Note the following revisions:

Wordy	*Better*
There are two reports on your desk.	Two reports are on your desk.
It is not important that you read every word.	You need not read every word.
Our supervisor is a person who is easy to work for.	Our supervisor is easy to work for.
The reason why she would not sign the letter is because she found two errors.	She would not sign the letter because she found two errors.
They tried a variety of different long-distance services.	They tried different long-distance services.
I wish that this day were over with!	I wish this day were over!
Due to the fact that he was habitually late, his supervisor put him on probation.	Because he was habitually late, his supervisor put him on probation.

Below are some more wordy phrases and alternatives:

Wordy	Alternatives
a long one	long
any and all, each and every, first and foremost	(use one of the pair)
cooperate together	cooperate
experience growth	grow
final outcome	outcome
for copying purposes, for the purpose of copying	for copying
give consideration to	consider
in an angry manner	angrily
information which is of a confidential nature	confidential information
in spite of the fact that	although
is of the opinion that	believes
make an inquiry regarding	inquire about
there is no doubt that	no doubt, doubtless
personal opinion	opinion
she is one who	she
the fact that he did not come	his absence
this is the one that is	this one is

very, really, completely (and many other vague adverbs)	(not necessary)
which is a great idea	a great idea
who is a good worker	a good worker
worthy of merit	meritorious

See also section 203i, page 24, for information on using common words. See section 323, page 64, for information on unnecessary prepositions.

g. Vary Sentence Length and Structure. As you edit, read your work aloud. Listen to your sentences and consider these questions:

- Do the sentences have similar structures?
- Are the sentences about the same length?
- Do the sentences sound monotonous?
- Is the same rhythm repeated without variety?

If you answer "Yes" to any of these questions, edit the sentences to vary their structure and length. When sentences are all written with the same structure and in the same length, your writing may sound dull.

Read the following paragraphs aloud, comparing their use of sentence variety:

Lacks Sentence Variety	*Sentences Vary*
Yesterday we met with the clients. We took them to lunch at Rhonda's. We talked about our new line of golf clubs. They seemed to be interested. We will call again next week. We think we can make a sale.	Yesterday we took the clients to lunch at Rhonda's to talk about our new line of golf clubs. They seemed interested, so we will call again next week. We think we can make a sale.

Here are some ways to vary your sentence length and structure:

- Connect two or more short sentences, for example:

Original: We took them to lunch at Rhonda's. We talked about our new line of golf clubs.

Rewrite: We took them to lunch at Rhonda's and talked about our new line of golf clubs.

See sections 418, page 87, and 433, page 103, for information on connecting main clauses with commas and semicolons.

- Break up long, compound sentences to form two or more shorter sentences, for example:

Original: We took them to lunch at Rhonda's to talk about our new line of golf clubs, and they seemed interested, so we will call them next week to follow up.

Rewrite: We took them to lunch at Rhonda's to talk about our new line of golf clubs. They seemed interested, so we will call them next week to follow up.

See section 203a, page 14, for information on complete sentences.

- Begin with something other than the subject of the sentence, such as a dependent clause, a prepositional phrase, or an adverb, for example:

Original: We took them to lunch at Rhonda's and talked about our new line of golf clubs.

Rewrite: Because we wanted more time to discuss our new line of golf clubs, we took them to lunch.

The editing strategy described in the TECH TIP after section 203a is especially useful for improving sentence variety. Once you have a list of sentences, you can glance at the list to ensure that sentence length varies. You can also check the beginnings of sentences; if many begin with their main subjects, perhaps you should rearrange some of them.

h. Use Active Voice Most of the Time. Good reasons exist for using passive-voice sentences (*see section 106, page 8*). Often, however, active-voice sentences are a better choice. Review any passive-voice sentences and consider whether you should edit to make them active. Compare the pairs below:

Passive	*Active*
Ms. Randall was promoted yesterday by Ms. Santos.	Ms. Santos promoted Ms. Randall yesterday.
Your paycheck will not be received for one month.	You will not receive your paycheck for one month.

See also section 106, page 8, on using the active voice.

i. Use Common Words. A large vocabulary increases your understanding of complex ideas. It also provides you more choices when writing, but you must choose intelligently. When you need a long, unfamiliar word to express an idea accurately, use it. When a shorter, more familiar word will do, use the more familiar word.

Most readers appreciate a simple, direct style in business writing. Compare the following sentences with their revisions:

Big Words	**Common Words**
Once you incorporate effective organizational behaviors, your productivity and efficiency will show significant improvement.	Once you are organized, your productivity will improve.
According to research findings, workers who take cognizance of the message they want to communicate and also consider their potential audience are definitely the most effective communicators.	According to research, workers who consider both their message and their reader communicate best.

See also section 203f, page 20, for information on removing unnecessary words.

j. Use Positive Language. Even if your letter is positive, your reader may view it negatively if you use too many negative words such as *no, not,* and *never.* As you edit sentences, look for negative words and rewrite as shown below:

Negative	**Positive**
Don't miss today's planning meeting.	Please attend today's planning meeting.
If you do not attend the sale, you cannot take advantage of our low prices.	If you come to the sale, you can benefit from our low prices.
We will not accept bids after Friday.	We will accept bids through Friday.

| Ms. Wilkins will not have time to see you until next week. | Ms. Wilkins will see you next week. |

k. Eliminate Bias from Your Writing. As you write, be sensitive to the feelings of others. Do not use language that may offend them or that discriminates against them. You may unintentionally use offensive language when you refer to people from different ethnic, racial, or religious groups; people from different generations; people with different sexual orientations; or people with physical limitations. The most common form of bias in writing occurs in references to men and women:

If Mr. Randall has an *office assistant,* please get *her* name.

Does the writer of this sentence mean to suggest that office assistants are all female? This assumption may offend both women and men. You may edit the offending sentence in various ways. Here are three possibilities:

Please get the name of Mr. Randall's office assistant.

What is the name of Mr. Randall's office assistant?

Who is Mr. Randall's office assistant?

Note: A good way to avoid gender bias is to pluralize references to people:

If Mr. Randall has any *assistants*, please get *their* names.

Below are other examples of possibly offensive references:

Possibly Offensive	*Better*
Leave your package with the old woman at the reception desk.	Leave your package with the receptionist.

Whenever a worker has a new idea, he contributes to our success.	Workers' new ideas contribute to our success.
Those Asians really understand computers. Let's assign her to research and development.	She's especially skilled with computers. Let's assign her to research and development.
This company has too may chiefs and not enough Indians!	This company has too many bosses and not enough workers!
We will use some of the men to help us move these boxes.	We will use volunteers to help us move these boxes.
I left that company because Simmons treated us like slaves.	I left that company because Simmons treated us badly.

See section 313d, page 49, for more information on gender-based pronoun usage.

Proofread Your Document 204

Once you are sure you have covered all the information you want to cover, organized the information effectively, and edited your sentences correctly, you are ready to proofread. Here are some common types of errors to watch for:

- Letter transpositions and other typographical errors
- Spelling and word choice errors
- Punctuation and capitalization errors
- Missing material (missing sentences, parts of sentences, paragraphs, or document parts)

- Grammatical errors
- Hyphenation errors
- Inconsistencies in mechanical details, such as abbreviations and the use of numbers and symbols

The number of errors you *could* make is endless. In reality, however, you probably make only a few kinds of errors—but make them repeatedly. If you record the kinds of errors you make, you will probably begin to see a pattern. Knowing this pattern can make future proofreading easier.

205 | Check the Appearance of Your Document

Some common errors in appearance are:

- Missing or extra space (for example, above and below headings or between paragraphs)
- Inconsistent alignment of margins and elements such as headers, footers, and columns
- Unbalanced page appearance

See sections 1002 (page 259), 1022–1025 (pages 281–284), and 1033 (page 303) for information on formatting letters, memos, and reports. See sections 1002, page 259, and 1030, page 294, for information on document formatting.

206 | Proofreaders' Marks

Proofreaders' marks are symbols used to indicate corrections when proofreading. Below are the most common marks in use today. These marks are especially useful when proofreading for another writer since most of the marks are well known. You may also find them useful in marking your own writing, particularly if you will not be correcting your errors immediately.

Mark	Meaning	Example
℘	Delete	The reasons is
Sp.	Spell out	Make ⑤ copies
tr	Transpose	information confidential
¶	New paragraph	pages. Finally, you will
no ¶	No paragraph	pages. Finally, you will
lc	Use lowercase	Along the Avenue
cap	Use capital letters	Along washburn avenue
◡	Close space	lower case letters
℘	Delete and close space	ommissions
#	Insert space	lowercase letters
=/=	Insert hyphen	easy to read instructions
bf	Set in boldface	lowercase letters
rom	Set in roman type	lowercase letters
‖	Align vertically	First, you must Next, you must
═	Align horizontally	Next you must
⊏	Move left	First, you must
⊐	Move right	Next, you must
stet	Let stand as originally written	Next, you must

Tech Tip

Spelling checkers and style checkers will help tremendously with your proofreading. Most word processing programs come with a spell checker and are compatible with commercially available style checkers. *See appendix E for more information on style checkers.*

NOTES

COMMON GRAMMAR AND USAGE PROBLEMS

- Subject-Verb Agreement
- Verbs
- Pronouns
- Adjectives and Adverbs
- Prepositions

PART THREE

NOTES

COMMON GRAMMAR AND USAGE PROBLEMS

SUBJECT-VERB AGREEMENT

An electronic style checker will often alert you to errors in subject-verb agreement. *See appendix E for more information on style checkers.*

Tech Tip

Singular or Plural Subject

301

In most cases, it is easy for you to write using correct subject-verb agreement. You determine whether the subject of your sentence is singular or plural and then use a verb that matches—that "agrees":

     s   v
The *machine runs* day and night. [Singular]

     s   v
The *machines run* day and night. [Plural]

Note: When determining subject-verb agreement, disregard parts of the sentence that come between the subject and verb:

     s   v
The *machines* by the door *run* day and night.

     s   v
The *president*, along with her advisors, *finds* the report helpful.

More Than One Subject Joined by *And*

Sometimes your sentence will have more than one subject (a compound subject) joined by the word *and.* A compound subject joined by *and* is plural:

          S   S   V

The security *guard* and the *manager meet* every Monday.

           S   S   S   V

The answering *machine,* the fax *machine,* and the *copier are* all easy to operate.

Note: Some subjects that appear to be compound are actually singular in meaning, for example:

    S   V

Wilson and Bowes is her favorite bank. [*Wilson and Bowes* is a company name.]

The *president and CEO*, Ms. Hicks, was here today. [The same person is both *president* and *CEO*.]

See section 307, page 39, for information on proper nouns that may appear plural.

More Than One Subject Joined by Other Connectors

Sometimes your sentence will have more than one subject (a compound subject) joined by words other than *and.* Such connectors might be:

or
nor
not only . . . but also
either . . . or
neither . . . nor

In cases such as these, the subject closer to the verb determines whether the verb is singular or plural:

          s   s   v
The warehouse *light* or the yard *lights stay* on all night.

            s   s   v
The yard *lights* or the warehouse *light stays* on all night.

               s   s   v
Neither the *mechanics* nor the maintenance *supervisor checks* the trucks for fuel.

        s   s v
Either *you* or *I am* responsible for locking up.

Sentences in Which the Verb Precedes the Subject   304

a. Sentences Beginning with *There Is/There Are* or *Here Is/Here Are*. When a sentence begins with the words *There* or *Here*, determining subject-verb agreement can be difficult. In these cases, the subject often follows the verb. *There* and *Here* are never subjects:

       v   s
There *are* two more *files* to review.

       v   s
Here *is* one *applicant* I would recommend.

       v   s
There's another copy *machine* in the next office.

b. Questions. If in doubt about whether the subject of a sentence that begins with a question is singular or plural, turn the sentence around:

$$\overset{\text{v}}{\text{Where }} \textit{is} \text{ the operations } \overset{\text{s}}{\textit{manual}?}$$

Where *is* the operations *manual*? [*The operations manual is where?*]

Does the spreadsheet *program work* well? (*Does work* is the complete verb.) [*The spreadsheet program does work well.*]

---

305 **Pronouns as Subjects**

a. Pronouns That Are Always Singular. Some pronouns are always considered singular when they act as the subject of the sentence. The most common of these pronouns are:

each	everyone
either	neither
everybody	one

Each of the assistants *has* a clear set of duties.

Everyone in the company *takes* a break between 11:00 and 1:00.

Neither of the managers *follows* that philosophy.

One of your coworkers *takes* vacation next week.

b. Pronouns That Are Always Plural. Some pronouns are always considered plural when they act as the subject of the sentence. The most common of these pronouns are:

both
few
many
several

s   v

Both of us *work* for Ms. Vang.

s   v

Few of the cars ever *sell* at sticker price.

s   v

Several of the sales reps *report* late each week.

See sections 313-317, pages 46-54, for more information on pronouns. See section 817, page 192, for information on possessive pronouns.

Subjects That Can Be Singular or Plural | 306 |

a. Pronouns That Can Be Singular or Plural. Some pronouns can be singular or plural, depending on the noun to which they refer. The most common of these pronouns are:

all
more
most
none
some

Singular

s   ref v
All the *filing is* finished.

s   ref   v
More of the *report remains* to be written.

s   ref
Some of the annual *report*
v
is easy to read.

Plural

s   ref v
All the *files are* here.

s   ref   v
More of the *reports remain* to be written.

s
Some of the annual
ref v
reports are easy to read.

b. Nouns That Name a Group. Nouns that name a group are called *collective nouns*. Collective nouns represent a single group made up of individual people or things. Since collective nouns refer to the group as a whole, they are usually singular. A few examples are:

        committee   management
        department   staff
        family   team
        group

          s   v
The *committee meets* at 2:00 tomorrow.

         s   v
Your *staff seems* very productive.

When you want to refer to the individual people or things rather than the group itself, rewrite your sentences. Then the collective nouns are no longer the subject:

                  s   v
The department *members argue* with each other at times.

        s   v
The *members* of your staff *seem* very productive.

See section 901, page 215, for a discussion of the word *data*.

c. Nouns That End with -*ics*. When nouns ending with -*ics* refer to a general body of knowledge or a general quality, they are usually singular. When they refer to the many facets of a body of knowledge or of a quality, they are usually plural. Some examples are:

        economics   mathematics
        ethics   politics
        graphics   statistics

General Body of Knowledge	Several Facets of a Topic
s v *Economics is* my favorite field of study.	s The *economics* of the situation v *are* hard to understand.
s v *Graphics is* one of the most interesting topics to learn.	s v Computer *graphics are* used a lot today.
s v *Mathematics is* an easy course to take.	s v The *statistics* she used *are* not clear.

Proper Nouns 307

Many proper nouns look plural because they are connected by *and* or because they end in *s*. In many cases, however, these proper nouns are singular. Here are some examples:

Company Names:	Gorman and Levers
	Brooks Brothers
Titles:	*Popular Mechanics*
	Consumer Reports
Countries:	United States

     s   v
Brooks Brothers is having a sale today!

     s   v
Consumer Reports is a widely read magazine.

   s v
Wales is a small and beautiful country.

See section 502, page 133, for information on distinguishing between common and proper nouns.

Sometimes subjects are not simple nouns but verb forms, phrases, or clauses acting as subjects. In these cases, the subject is singular:

              s   v
Effective *managing is* an art.

   s   v
Managing the office *is* difficult work.

         s   v
Maria's *quitting made* us unhappy. [*See section 818, page 193, for information on using possessives before -ing words.*]

        s   v
To key 90 words per minute is exceptional.

           s   v
Whoever manages the office well has my respect.

        s   v
What the boss wants is two new policy statements.

       s   v
What the boss wants is one more sales rep for this territory.

but

     s (compound)   v
Saving money and *using it wisely are* good consumer skills.

See section 417d, page 86, for more information on phrases and clauses as subjects of sentences. See section 422a, page 93, for information on separating subjects from their verbs with commas.

The simple past, present, and future tenses indicate that something *happened, happens* (or *is happening*), or *will happen*; however, the perfect tenses indicate more complex time relationships. The following guidelines will help you decide when to use a perfect-tense verb.

a. Present Perfect Tense. This tense indicates that some action began in the past and either continues in the present or has recently been completed. Note that the helping verbs *has* and *have* are used *(see section 310, page 42):*

She *has needed* a good computer network since we expanded. [Action began in the past and continues in the present.]

We *have seen* all the people we need. [Action began in the past and was recently completed.]

b. Past Perfect Tense. This tense indicates that an action was completed before a certain time in the past. Note that the helping verb *had* is used *(see section 310, page 42):*

The group *had* already *eaten* when Ed arrived. [Ed arrived, but the group finished eating before Ed arrived.]

Roxanne *had* just *left* when the news was announced. [The news was announced, but Roxanne left before the announcement.]

c. Future Perfect Tense. This tense indicates that some action will be completed by some specific time in the future. Note that the helping verb phrase *will have* is used *(see section 310, page 42):*

By the time you arrive, your friend *will have forgotten*. [Your friend will forget at some time in the future, that is, by the time you arrive.]

When you reach 65, you *will have earned* your pension. [You will earn your pension at some time in the future, that is, when you reach 65.]

---

310 | Forms of Difficult Verbs

On occasion, speakers and writers use the wrong verb forms to express their thoughts. Most commonly, speakers and writers who want to use a perfect tense mistakenly combine helping verbs with past tense forms instead of the correct past participle. The table below shows the present tense, the past tense, and the past participle of the most common difficult verbs. Following the table are examples of both correct and incorrect use of the perfect tense of difficult verbs:

Present Tense	*Past Tense*	*Past Participle*
		(used with helping verbs *has, have,* or *had)*
am	was	been
are	were	been
begin	began	begun
bring	brought	brought
choose	chose	chosen
come	came	come
do	did	done
eat	ate	eaten
get	got	gotten/got
give	gave	given

Present Tense	Past Tense	Past Participle
go	went	gone
grow	grew	grown
is	was	been
lay	laid	laid
lie	lay	lain
rise	rose	risen
see	saw	seen
set	set	set
sit	sat	sat
speak	spoke	spoken
teach	taught	taught
wear	wore	worn
write	wrote	written

Wrong	Rewrite
This person *has came* to check the laser printer.	This person *has come* to check the laser printer.
I *have* never *ate* lunch in the office cafeteria before.	I *have* never *eaten* lunch in the office cafeteria before.
I'm sorry, but he *has went* for the day.	I'm sorry, but he *has gone* for the day.
I should *have wrote* the letter yesterday.	I should *have written* the letter yesterday.

See section 901, pages 201–236, for a discussion of difficult verb pairs such as *lie* and *lay*.

Some electronic style checkers will alert you to incorrectly used verb forms and other word problems. *See appendix E for more information on style checkers.*

---

311 | **Verb Form in Wishes, Recommendations, Demands, and Conditions Contrary to Fact**

In the situations described below, use the *subjunctive form* (mood) of the verb. In the examples provided, notice how the *subjunctive form* most often differs from the form used regularly (i.e., the *indicative form*). *See appendix D for verb form definitions.*

Past Tense Changes:	*Were* is used for both singular and plural subjects.
	Had replaces *have* in verb phrases such as *have been* and *have gone.*
Present Tense Changes:	The plural form of the verb (e.g., *take* instead of *takes*) is used for both singular and plural
	Be is used instead of *am, are*, and *is.*

a. Wishes, Recommendations, and Demands.   Use the *subjunctive* form of the verb when expressing wishes, recommendations, and demands in clauses that begin with the word *that*:

I wish that I *were* taking vacation next week.

I recommend that you *be* promoted immediately.

I demand that he *take* a lunch break each day.

Note: In some sentences *that* is *understood*; in other words, it does not actually appear in the sentence:

I wish (that) I *were* taking vacation next week.

See sections 414c, page 80, and 901, page 232, for more information on clauses beginning with *that*.

b. Conditions Contrary to Fact. When referring to situations that are not true or are hypothetical (i.e., not true, but discussed as if they were true), use the *subjunctive* verb form. Such expressions usually begin with the word *if*:

If he *were paid* more, he might be more motivated.

If she *were* the manager, the office might run more smoothly.

I would take the day off if she *were* here.

I would be promoted tomorrow if I *had gone* to training.

Note: Not all clauses beginning with *if* express situations that are not true or are hypothetical. In the following sentences, the subjunctive would be incorrect:

If he was sick yesterday, he should not have come to work. [He probably was sick.]

If you go to the reception desk, please pick up that package for me. [You might go to the reception desk. If you do, please pick up that package.]

See section 901, page 219, for information on the distinction between *if* and *whether*.

312 | Splitting Infinitive Phrases

An infinitive phrase is a phrase that begins with the word *to* and is followed by a verb: *to go, to sell merchandise, to key data,* and so on. Do not separate *to* from its verb with a lengthy modifier:

Wrong: She wanted *to, within the hour, plan* the next steps.

Wrong: He found a way *to more thoroughly and effectively prepare* his assistants.

Note: When the modifier is short (a word or two), splitting the infinitive phrase is not confusing and often sounds natural:

She wanted *to quickly plan* the next steps.

He found a way *to better prepare* his assistants for their office duties.

PRONOUNS

Pronouns are used to refer to nouns, to other pronouns, or to phrases and clauses serving as nouns.

313 | Pronoun-Reference Agreement

Each pronoun must match, or agree with, the other word or group of words to which it refers (i.e., its *reference* or *antecedent*). There are two kinds of agreement needed between pronouns and their references: agreement in *number* (singular or plural) and agreement in *gender* (male, female, or neutral):

a. Singular and Plural Pronoun-Reference Agreement.
A pronoun and its antecedent must both be singular, or they must both be plural:

	ref pn
Wrong:	*Each group member* must bring *their* notes to the meeting. [*Member* is singular, but *their* is plural.]

	ref pn
Rewrite:	*Each group member* must bring *his or her* notes to the meeting. [Both singular.]

or

          ref   pn
All group members must bring *their* notes to the meeting. [Both plural.]

	ref pn
Wrong:	*Everybody* must clear *their* own desk each day. [*Everybody* is singular but *their* is plural.]

	ref pn
Rewrite:	*Everybody* must clear *his or her* own desk each day. [Both singular.]

or

          ref   pn
All *employees* must clear *their* own desks each day. [Both plural.]

Note: Making references and pronouns plural helps avoid awkward phrases such as *his or her. See section 313d, page 49, for a discussion of gender-neutral pronouns and references.*

More examples:

          ref   pn
The *company* purchased *its* new computer network yesterday. [Both singular.]

```
ref                                      pn
```
Each of the managers must prepare *his or her* own schedule. [Both singular.]

```
                    ref          pn
```
The committee *members* brought *their* budget notes to every meeting. [Both plural.]

```
           ref          pn
```
When our *assistants* come in, *they* will find a surprise. [Both plural.]

See section 305a–b, pages 36–37, for pronouns that are always singular or always plural when they act as subjects. See section 203d, page 18, for information on editing sentences to ensure clear pronoun references.

b. Pronouns with More Than One Reference Joined by And. When a pronoun's reference is more than one noun or pronoun joined by the word *and*, the reference is plural and the pronoun should be plural:

```
           ref                        pn
```
Ms. Templeton and I would like you to see *our* point of view this time.

```
           ref                           pn
```
Jane and I would like to meet with you this week, and *we* have every afternoon free.

```
           ref                            pn
```
Ms. Smith and her assistant met yesterday. *They* said the meeting was very productive.

```
           ref                  pn
```
Bob and Enrique will be happy with *their* promotions.

See section 307, page 39, for possible exceptions to this rule.

c. Pronouns with More Than One Reference Joined by Or. At times a pronoun's reference is more than one noun or pronoun joined by the words *or* or *nor*. In these cases, the pronoun should agree with the nearer reference in number (singular or plural):

<pre>
        ref   pn
Either <i>Kai</i> or <i>John</i> must present <i>his</i> ideas first.
</pre>

<pre>
             ref   pn
Neither <i>Mary</i> nor <i>her assistants</i> may take <i>their</i> break right
now.
</pre>

<pre>
                ref   pn
Neither <i>Mary's assistants nor she</i> may take <i>her</i> break right
</pre>
now. [This sentence sounds awkward. Rewrite it as in the previous sentence.]

d. Pronoun-Reference Agreement in Gender. A pronoun and its reference must both be male, female, or neutral:

<pre>
      ref   pn
Mr. Williams leaves his office each day at 6:00. [Both male.]
</pre>

<pre>
      ref   pn
Ms. Fontana opens her doors at 8:00 every morning. [Both
female.]
</pre>

<pre>
        ref   pn
Every <i>company</i> must balance <i>its</i> books. [Both neutral.]
</pre>

Many nouns do not definitely refer to males or to females. For example, *manager, employee, mechanic, secretary, assistant, supervisor,* and many others can refer to males, to females, or to both males and females. A few pronouns are similarly indefinite with regard to gender: *one, each, every, everybody, either, neither, somebody,* and so on. When using pronouns that refer to such gender-neutral nouns and pronouns, never assume the gender. Instead, you have three options:

1. Use pronouns that represent both genders, such as *he or she, she or he, him or her, her or his*, and so on.

2. Make your noun plural and use *they* and *their*.

3. Rewrite your sentence to avoid the problem.

For example:

Wrong: When we find a new *doctor*, *he* will no doubt be well qualified.

Rewrite: When we find a new *doctor*, *he or she* will no doubt be well qualified.

                or

           Any new doctor we find will no doubt be well qualified.

Wrong: Any *nurse* who works in corporate health knows *she* is making good money.

Rewrite: *Nurses* who work in corporate health know *they* are making good money.

Wrong: *Everybody* wants *his* work station to be comfortable.

Rewrite: *Everybody* wants *his or her* work station to be comfortable.

                or

           All workers want comfortable workstations.

See section 203d, page 18, for information on clear pronoun reference. See section 203k, page 26, for information on eliminating bias from your writing.

Pronouns are classified by *case*. English has three major pronoun cases: the *nominative* case (pronoun used as subject), the *objective* case (pronoun used as object), and the *possessive* case (pronoun showing possession). Here are examples of the three cases:

Nominative	Objective	Possessive
I	me	my, mine
he/she	him/her	his/her/hers
it	it	its
you	you	your/yours
we	us	our/ours
they	them	their/theirs
who	whom	whose

See section 901, pages 201–251, for a discussion of *it's/its, who/whom, that/which/who/whose,* and *their/there/they're.* See section 817, page 192, for more information on possessive pronouns. See section 317, page 54, for pronouns in the reflexive case, i.e., pronouns that end with *-self.*

a. Pronouns as Subjects. Use the nominative case for pronouns that function as subjects in a sentence. Also, use the same case for two or more pronouns that fill the same role in a sentence:

Wrong:　　　*Him* and *I* should work together sometime. *[Him* and *I* are subjects, but *him* is in the objective case.]

Rewrite:　　　He and *I* should work together some time.

Wrong:	Phong and *me* had lunch together. [*Me* is part of the subject but is in the objective case.]
Rewrite:	Phong and *I* had lunch together.

Wrong:	*Us assistants* are taking a break. [*Assistants* is the subject, and *Us* refers to that subject. Use the nominative *we* instead.]
Rewrite:	*We* assistants are taking a break.

b. Pronouns as Objects. Use the objective case for pronouns that function as objects in a sentence, including pronouns used as objects of a preposition. Use the same case for two or more pronouns that fill the same role in a sentence:

Wrong:	Between *you* and *I*, Mike is going to get the promotion.
Rewrite:	Between *you* and *me*, Mike is going to get the promotion.

Hint: To determine the correct case of a pronoun that appears with another pronoun or a noun, do this: Delete one of the pair and say the other aloud in the sentence. Your experience will usually tell you which choice is correct, for example:

Original Sentence:	They left the office with Sheila and *I/me*.
Say aloud:	They left the office with *I*. They left the office with *me*. [*Me* is correct in this case.]

More examples:

Wrong:	They left the office with *her* and *I*. [*Her* and *I* are both objects of the preposition *with*, but *I* is in the nominative case.]
Rewrite:	They left the office with *her* and *me*. [Both *her* and *me* are objects of the preposition *with* and both are in the objective case.]

Wrong:	He typed the report for Jane and *I*.
Rewrite:	He typed the report for Jane and *me*.

Wrong:	Come to the cafeteria with Josh and *I*.
Rewrite:	Come to the cafeteria with Josh and *me*.

Pronouns after Forms of the Verb *To Be* 315

In very formal writing, use the nominative case of pronouns after verbs such as *is*, *are*, *am*, *was*, *were*, *been*, and *being*:

Wrong:	It was *me* who called.
Rewrite:	It was *I* who called.
Wrong:	Is it *her* you need?
Rewrite:	Is it *she* you need?

Note: Many informed speakers of English do not follow this rule in casual conversations.

See section 318d, page 57, for information on adjectives and adverbs following forms of *be*.

Pronouns in Comparisons with *Than* and *As*. 316

When making comparisons, be sure your sentence actually compares the items intended. Using the wrong form of the pronoun can lead to faulty comparisons:

Wrong:	Sandy can sell *better than him*. [Compares unlike things—Sandy's ability to sell with *him*.]
Rewrite:	Sandy can sell *better than he*. [Compares like things—Sandy's ability to sell with someone else's ability to sell. *Can sell* is not written after *he* but is understood.]

Note: The correct pronoun in the previous sentence (*he*) is in the nominative case because the full phrases are being compared: *Sandy can sell* compared with *he can sell*. Compared items are always in the same case.

More examples:

I like her better than him. [*Her* and *him* are being compared.]

I like her better than he does. [*I like her* is being compared to *he likes her*. *Does* merely substitutes for *likes*.]

Note: Writers and speakers often leave one or more of the last words out of the sentence when the comparison involves two phrases. Cutting the last phrase short is all right as long as the comparison remains clear, for example:

Sandy can sell better than he can [sell].

I like her better than he does [like her].

He can key faster than I [can key].

My boss is taller than I [am tall].

If your desk chair is higher than mine [is high], we can trade.

See section 901, pages 208 and 215, for the distinction between *different from* and *different than* and between *like* and *as*.

| 317 | **Pronouns That End in *-self*** |

Pronouns such as *himself, herself,* and *themselves* are called *reflexive pronouns*. Use reflexive pronouns in two situations only:

1. To emphasize the noun (or pronoun) to which they refer:

   The *employees themselves* ran the office while the management team was away.

Never mind. *I* will do it *myself.*

2. To direct the action back to the subject of the sentence:

I cannot give *myself* credit for that work.

You should all congratulate *yourselves* on a job
well done.

The most common error writers and speakers make with
reflexive pronouns is to use them in place of objective pronouns:

Wrong:	Return the signed copy to Mike or *myself* by Friday.
Rewrite:	Return the signed copy to Mike or *me* by Friday.

Wrong:	Georgia, the attached form must be signed by Monique or *yourself.*
Rewrite:	Georgia, the attached form must be signed by Monique or *you.*

See section 314, page 51, for other forms (cases) of pronouns.

ADJECTIVES AND ADVERBS

Using Adjectives and Adverbs Correctly 318

Adjectives and adverbs are modifiers. That is, they provide
more information about other words in a sentence. Adjectives
modify nouns and pronouns. Adverbs modify verbs, adjectives,
and other adverbs.

a. Adjectives.

The *tall* manager is new this year. [*Tall* modifies *manager.*]

The manager is *effective*. [*Effective* modifies *manager.*]

She is very *productive*. [*Productive* modifies *she*.]

Finding time to exercise is *easy*. [*Easy* modifies the noun phrase *Finding time to exercise*.]

b. Adverbs.

The accountant *quickly* calculated the deductions. [*Quickly* modifies the verb *calculated*.]

The manager is *extremely* effective. [*Extremely* modifies the adjective *effective*.]

The accountant calculated the deductions *very* quickly. [*Very* modifies the other adverb *quickly*.]

See section 203c, page 17, for information on placing modifiers to clearly relate to the words they modify.

c. Adjective and Adverb Forms. Because they both modify, adjectives and adverbs are sometimes confused. Writers may use adverb forms instead of adjective forms and adjective forms instead of adverb forms. Your dictionary will help you with difficult adjective and adverb forms, some of which follow:

Adjective	*Adverb*
bad	badly
busy	busily
cheap	cheap/cheaply
close	close/closely
costly	——
daily	daily
early	early
fair	fair/fairly
fast	fast
former	formerly
friendly	——
good	well
hard	hardly

Adjective	Adverb
——	here
hourly	hourly
important	importantly
last	last
late	late/lately
lively	——
lonely	——
loud	loud/loudly
lovely	——
monthly	monthly
——	never
no	not
only	only
past	past
quick	quick/quickly
real	really
right	right/rightly
short	short/shortly
similar	similarly
slow	slow/slowly
strong	strongly
——	then
——	there
timely	——
——	too
usual	usually
——	very
weekly	weekly
whole	wholly
wrong	wrong/wrongly
yearly	yearly

d. Adjectives and Adverbs after Forms of the Verb *Be*.
Writers commonly confuse adjective and adverb forms after
forms of the verb *to be (is, are, been*, etc.). The same problem
often occurs after verbs such as *appear, become, feel* (when

referring to the state of one's health or to emotion), *look*, *remain*, *seem*, *smell*, *sound*, *taste*, and *turn*:

Wrong:	She looks busily. [*Busily* modifies the pronoun *She* and, therefore, should be the adjective *busy*.]
Rewrite:	She looks busy.

Wrong:	He feels badly for her. [*Badly* modifies the pronoun *He* and, therefore, should be the adjective *bad*.]
Rewrite:	He feels bad for her.

See section 901, page 209, for a discussion of *bad* and *badly*. See section 315, page 53, for information on pronouns following forms of *to be*.

---

319 | Using Adjectives and Adverbs to Compare

Different forms of adjectives and adverbs are used to compare two or more things:

a. Comparing Two Things. When comparing two things with adjectives or adverbs, use the comparative form of the modifier. To form the comparative, either add *-er* to the word or modify the word with *more* (see Note that follows):

Modifier	*Comparative Form*	*Superlative Form*
great	greater	greatest
soon	sooner	soonest
profitable	more profitable	most profitable
quickly	more quickly	most quickly

For example:

Wrong: This is the *greatest* of the two numbers.

Rewrite: This is the *greater* of the two numbers.

Wrong: Which of you two has the *highest* salary?

Rewrite: Which of you two has the *higher* salary?

Wrong: Of the two letters, which is *most* legible?

Rewrite: Of the two letters, which is *more* legible?

Note: Often, you add *-er* to form the comparative of single-syllable words and use *more* to form the comparative of words of two or more syllables. Since this is not always true, however, check your dictionary if you are in doubt.

b. Comparing Three or More Things. When comparing three or more things with adjectives or adverbs, use the *superlative* form of the modifier. You form the superlative by adding *-est* to the word or modifying the word with *most*:

Modifier	Comparative Form	Superlative Form
great	greater	greatest
soon	sooner	soonest
profitable	more profitable	most profitable
quickly	more quickly	most quickly

For example:

Of all the mail carriers, she is the *fastest*.

Last year, we had our *highest* sales in the third quarter.

She is the *most impressive* applicant I have interviewed so far.

That is the *most affordable* copier on the market.

Note: Often, you form the superlative of single-syllable words by adding *-est* and form the superlative of words of two or more syllables by using *most*. Since this is not always true, however, check your dictionary if you are in doubt.

c. Irregular Comparatives and Superlatives. Some adjectives and adverbs do not form their comparative and superlative forms as described above. Here are some common examples:

Modifier	*Comparative*	*Superlative*
bad	worse	worst
good/well	better	best
little (degree)	less/lesser	least
many/much	more	most

For example:

My report was *bad*, but his was *worse*.

Are you doing *better* than you did yesterday?

Ralph took *little* care when keying, and I took even *less*. Bridget took the *least*.

If you have *much* trouble or *many* complaints, you can be sure that Janice will have *more* and Darrell will have the *most*.

No, not, never, nothing, and *neither* are negative words. Double negatives usually cancel each other out. Notice that adding a second negative in each of the sentences below reverses the meaning of the sentences:

Single Negative	***Double Negative***
Neither of the assistants will work hard.	*Neither* of the assistants will *not* work hard. [Means: Both will work hard.]
We can*not* do anything to help.	We can*not* do *nothing* to help. [Means: We can do something to help.]
I am *not* concerned about new shipments arriving today.	I am *not* *un*concerned about new shipments arriving today. [Means: I am concerned... .]

Note: Using double negatives is sometimes correct, as in the two "original" sentences below. However, rewriting the sentences to avoid the negatives will often make the sentences more direct and clear:

Original: I am *not* *un*concerned about new shipments arriving today.

Rewrite: I am concerned about new shipments arriving today.

Original: The data in the report is *not* *in*correct.

Rewrite: The data in the report is correct.

See also sections 203j, page 25, and 203f, page 20, for information on using positive language and removing unnecessary words.

PREPOSITIONS

| 321 | **Using Prepositions Correctly**

Prepositions are words that connect and show a relationship between two other sentence parts (*see appendix D*). *They always function as part of a prepositional phrase:*

     p
Please, come *into my office.*

 p
In three days, we begin production.

       p
My parking spot is *between hers and his.*

       p
We do our best *during July.*

    p
Because of you, I received the award.

       p
Can we meet them *after work?*

 p   p
Since yesterday, we have been waiting *for the call.*

 p
Of the three options, the management restructuring seems to be the most practical.

Note: Do not confuse prepositions with adverbs, which do not introduce a phrase but stand alone and modify adjectives and verbs. The same words frequently serve as both prepositions and adverbs:

Prepositions	*Adverbs*
p Jorge came *down the stairs.*	Jorge sat *down.* [Modifies *sat.*]
p Put those *in the file cabinet.*	Please, come *in.* [Modifies *come.*]
p She's really moving *up the corporate ladder.*	Place the award *up* there on the shelf. [Modifies *there.*]

See *in/into* in section 901, page 219, for more examples of the same words functioning as both prepositions and adverbs.

Prepositions at the End of Sentences 322

In the most formal writing, avoid ending sentences with prepositions. In ordinary usage, however, ending sentences with prepositions is acceptable:

What are the principles most organizations adhere *to*? [To what principles do most organizations adhere?]

Those marketing plans represent ideas we can experiment with. [Those marketing plans represent ideas with which we can experiment.]

323 | Unnecessary Prepositions

Some prepositions are unnecessary. If you can remove a preposition without changing the meaning or making the sentence less clear, remove it:

Where will we eat ~~at~~ today?

What time do you get off ~~of~~ work?

All ~~of~~ my coworkers worked on Saturday.

I wish this project were over ~~with~~.

324 | Troublesome Prepositions

Some verbs require the use of specific prepositions in specific situations (e.g., you *agree with* a person but *agree to* a plan). Also, some writers fail to observe the proper distinction between closely related prepositions such as *in* and *into* and *between* and *among*. Finally, certain prepositions are often used incorrectly as connectives. Section 901 offers usage guidelines on the most frequently misused prepositions.

PUNCTUATION

- Period
- Question Mark
- Exclamation Point
- Comma
- Apostrophe
- Colon
- Semicolon
- Quotation Marks
- Dash
- Parentheses
- Underline and Italics
- Hyphen

PART FOUR

NOTES

PUNCTUATION

PERIOD

At End of Sentence 401

Use a period at the end of a sentence that does not take a
question mark or an exclamation point:

Our office assistants attended the meeting.

Go to the accounting office to verify your social security number.

This rule includes polite requests and indirect questions. Polite
requests and indirect questions are those for which an answer
is not required:

Martina's question was whether health benefits applied to an
employee's dependents.

Would you return the enclosed copy with your signature.

Please attend the meeting if at all possible.

May I suggest that you call Customer Service with your
complaint.

Fred asked whether you were coming tomorrow.

Note: If an abbreviation ends a sentence, do not include a second period at the end of that sentence:

She works for MacMillan, Inc.

See section 441, page 110, for information on the use of periods with quotation marks.

Period Spacing. When typing, use two spaces between a period that ends a sentence and the first letter of the next sentence. Many word processing programs, however, print with *proportional spacing*, which is spacing that accounts for the differences in character sizes. When printing with proportional spacing, use only one space after sentence-ending periods.

---

402 | With Letters and Numbers in Outlines

Use a period after numbers and letters designating items in an outline:

PRESENTATION OUTLINE

I. Introduction

II. Project history

   A. Before Simmons began

      1. Undefined goals

      2. Poor planning

      3. Unmanageable process

B. After Simmons began

   1. Returned to planning stage

   2. Simplified process

  ` 3. Oversaw process carefully

III. Goals for next phase of project

Period Spacing in Outlines. The visual appearance of outlines is important. Periods and the items they introduce should align vertically, as in the example above. Note that to maintain proper alignment after the periods, you must key III, the longest of the roman numerals, two spaces to the left of I. This requires advance planning when setting your left margin. Alternatively, you can use a decimal tab to align the periods after letters and numbers.

8.

9.

10.

11.

See section 1034, page 306, for information on preparing and formatting outlines. See section 501d, page 132, for information on capitalizing outline entries.

After Letters and Numbers in Lists   403

Generally, use periods after letters or numbers that introduce items in a list:

We have three questions regarding your proposal:

1. Can you meet the deadline we have set?

2. Does your company have the necessary resources to complete each step of the process?

3. Can your company offer long-term maintenance?

Our four goals for the coming sales season are:

- Increased profits
- Decreased breakage and theft
- Decreased worker absence
- Increased worker morale

Note: Do not use periods with bullets or other stylistic symbols that introduce items in a list.

See section 501c, page 131, for information on capitalizing listed items. See section 428b, page 99, for more information on creating vertical lists.

___

<table>
<tr><td>404</td><td>**With Items in Lists**</td></tr>
</table>

Use periods at the end of listed items if the listed items are complete sentences. If the listed items are not complete sentences, use no end punctuation:

Everyone knows three things about our company:

1. We provide the lowest prices in the region.
2. We give our service technicians the most detailed training.
3. We offer the best warranties in the country.

Among the reasons for hiring her were:

a. Her extensive sales experience
b. Her management potential
c. Her positive approach to sales

See section 403, page 69, for information on punctuating letters and numbers introducing listed items. See sections 428b, page 99, and 501c, page 131, for information on introducing vertical lists with colons and for related capitalization rules.

As Decimal Point
405

Use periods (with no spacing) as decimal points in numbers:

5.7

89.2 percent

$45.95

See section 603, page 149, on using numbers and decimals to express money amounts.

In Abbreviations
406

See Part 7: Abbreviations for information on using periods with abbreviations.

QUESTION MARK

End of Question
407

Use a question mark at the end of direct questions:

When are the end-of-quarter reports due?

Did you know that she was promoted to assistant manager?

Who will read the applications, interview the candidates, and make final decisions?

When did Mr. Williamson ever say, "I'm sorry"?

See section 443, page 113, for more information on question marks with quotation marks. See section 401, page 67, for information on using periods to end polite requests and indirect questions.

Tech Tip

Question Mark Spacing. When typing, use two spaces after question marks that end sentences. Many word processing programs, however, print with *proportional spacing*, which is spacing that accounts for the differences in character sizes. When printing with proportional spacing, use only one space after question marks.

| 408 | **Questions within a Statement** |

Use a question mark at the end of a statement that contains a direct question:

The budget for the project will be increased, *won't it?*

We can carry over five vacation days, *can't we*, at the end of each year?

Tell me: *When will I have the data I ordered?*

See section 443, page 113, for information on using quotation marks for a question within a sentence.

EXCLAMATION POINT

Use the exclamation point to add emotion or emphasis to selected statements. If you overuse exclamation points, they lose their impact on the reader, so use them sparingly.

| 409 | **To Signal Strong Feelings** |

You can use exclamation marks at the end of sentences to signal strong feelings, such as eagerness, enthusiasm, joy, disbelief, urgency, or anger:

I'm so glad you could finally come!

I was shocked by that statement!

Note: When you wish to signal strong feelings in a question, use both the question mark and exclamation point:

What do you mean by that?!

In Stand-Alone Words and Phrases 410

Exclamation points are often used with single words or phrases to suggest, rather than state, complete thoughts:

Congratulations!

Unbelievable!

Absolutely not!

Yes!

See section 443, page 113, for information on using quotation marks with exclamation points.

COMMA

The comma is probably the most versatile punctuation mark in English. For this reason, commas are also the most overused and misused. Note that commas have three basic purposes:

- To set off elements within a sentence (two commas)
- To separate an element that begins or ends a sentence (one comma)
- To clarify meaning (one or two commas)

Commas That Set Off Sentence Elements

| 411 | In Direct Personal Address |

When addressing someone in a sentence, use commas to set off the name of the person you address:

> Now that you have completed the marketing course, *Bob,* could you handle the Rolls account for me?

> Please write the policy memo, *Rita,* so that I can distribute it to the sales representatives.

> Can you find time on your schedule, *Mr. Price,* to talk about next week? [The comma before Mr. Price serves two purposes: First, it helps set off the direct address from the rest of the sentence. Second, it separates the introductory clause from the clause that follows *(see section 417b, page 84).*]

| 412 | With Interrupting Words, Phrases, and Clauses |

Use commas to set off nonessential sentence elements that interrupt the main flow of the sentence:

a. Words. Set off words that interrupt the main flow of a sentence. These words are often transitional words or insertions of the writer's opinion, for example:

Transitions	*Insertions*
also	actually
consequently	apparently
conversely	frankly
finally	ideally
furthermore	incidentally
generally	perhaps
however	personally
instead	presumably
moreover	theoretically
therefore	unfortunately
too	

It could be, *also*, that he was not feeling well.

I would still, *however*, like to wait on that question.

We must agree, *therefore*, not to discuss this issue.

We·should, *ideally*, call Ms. Rost to the meeting.

I must say that I, *personally*, did not enjoy the seminar.

See section 411, page 74, for information on setting off direct personal addresses.

Note: Sentences with single-word interrupting elements are sometimes smoother if the interrupting element comes at the beginning or end of the sentence:

Therefore, we must all agree not to discuss this issue.

Ideally, we should call Ms. Rost to the meeting.

I would still like to wait on that question, *however*.

See section 417, page 83, for information on separating introductory elements from the rest of the sentence.

b. Phrases. Set off phrases that interrupt the main flow of the sentence. These interrupting phrases are generally transitional expressions or insertions of the writer's opinion, for example:

Transitions	*Insertions*
after all	as a matter of fact
as a result	if necessary
as a rule	if possible
at first	in fact

by contrast	in my opinion
by the way	of course
for example	to be honest
in addition	to say the least
in any case	to tell the truth
on one hand	to begin with
on the other hand	

They will, *on the other hand,* be providing free services.

Nancy's speech was, *by contrast,* quite interesting.

We can, *for example,* find out who has the best price.

Jacques was, *to tell the truth,* a great assistant.

Randy and Wilma must, *of course,* be included.

See section 414c, page 80, for information on setting off phrases that introduce phrases or clauses. See section 417b, page 84, for information on using a comma to separate introductory phrases and clauses.

c. Clauses. Set off clauses that interrupt the main flow of the sentence. These interrupting clauses may be insertions of the writer's opinion:

> as I see it
> as you know
> believe it or not
> I believe
> if I may
> if I may be honest
> if I must say
> or so I was told

He was, *as I see it,* the best manager we had.

Frank was, *I believe,* the only man in the department.

See sections 447 and 449, pages 118 and 119, for information on using dashes and parentheses to set off interrupting elements.

With Contrasting Expressions

Use commas to set off phrases that contrast two ideas. The word *not* usually appears in these phrases:

Please have two copies of the report, *not one*, ready for the evaluation team.

He was saddened, *but not surprised*, by her retirement.

She was in favor of, *not in opposition to*, the proposal. [Note that the commas do not set off elements that are essential to the sentence, such as the word *of*.]

With Nonessential Modifiers

Modifiers may be *essential* or *nonessential* to the basic meaning of the sentence.

Nonessential modifiers *describe* or *add information* about the element they modify; therefore, they are not essential to the meaning of a sentence. The message would be clear without them. Nonessential modifiers are usually set off from the rest of the sentence by commas.

Essential modifiers *define* or *distinguish* the element they modify; therefore, they are necessary to the meaning of the sentence. Essential modifiers are not set off by commas.

One way to test whether a modifier is essential is to remove it from the sentence and ask whether the basic sentence meaning remains; if a modifier can be removed, it is not essential and should be set off by commas.

a. Words. Single words can sometimes function as both essential and nonessential modifiers. These words are often appositives (nouns or noun phrases modifying other nouns):

Nonessential: My uncle, *Pat,* started this business.

This sentence implies that the writer has one uncle; therefore, the word *Pat* is not used to define which uncle but only to add information. With or without the name *Pat,* the emphasis is on *uncle.* Thus, the appositive *Pat* is nonessential.

Essential: My uncle *Pat* started this business.

This sentence implies that the writer has more than one uncle. For the reader to know which uncle started the business, the writer must include the name *Pat. Pat* defines *uncle* by clarifying which uncle is meant; therefore, *Pat* is essential to the meaning of the sentence.

Note: When using an appositive as part of a series of two or more items, make sure you clarify that the appositive is not a separate item in the series:

Unclear: Ramona, my boss, and I worked late. [Two or three people?]

Rewrite: Ramona (my boss) and I worked late.

See section 420c, page 91, for information on setting off a series of adjectives that follow the noun they modify.

b. Phrases. Modifying phrases can give either essential or nonessential information about a preceding noun or pronoun:

Nonessential: The annex, *built in 1990,* houses all our old records.

This sentence implies that there is only one annex. The phrase *built in 1990* does not define which annex the writer means; it merely gives information about the annex. Thus, the phrase is nonessential.

Essential: The annex *built in 1990* houses all our old records.

This sentence implies that more than one annex exists. The one *built in 1990* houses the records. *Built in 1990* is, therefore, essential to define which annex the writer means.

Nonessential: The new employee, waiting outside the controller's door, worried about his late paycheck.

This sentence implies that only one new employee exists. The phrase *waiting outside the controller's door* is nonessential; it can be removed without affecting the basic meaning of the sentence.

Essential: The new employee waiting outside the controller's door worried about his late paycheck.

This sentence implies that more than one new employee exists but only one of them is *waiting outside the controller's door*. The phrase *waiting outside the controller's door* is essential; it cannot be removed without affecting the basic meaning of the sentence, because it defines which employee is being discussed.

Nonessential: I should hire several new workers, *including an assistant and a receptionist*, before the end of January.

There are a few things we can do, *such as cutting back on returns, increasing customer service, and studying the market better*, before next year's evaluations.

See sections 412b, page 75, and 413, page 77, for information on setting off interrupting phrases, and contrasting expressions.

c. Clauses. Modifying clauses can give either essential or nonessential information. Clauses beginning with *that*, *which*, and *who* are especially common as modifiers, although many other clauses function as modifiers as well:

Nonessential: The Bates file, *which I could not find,* is the one I need for our meeting.

This sentence implies that there is only one Bates file. The *which* clause merely gives information about the Bates file. The reader would know which file the writer meant without the *which* clause. Thus, the *which* clause is nonessential.

Essential: The file *that Robert borrowed* is the one I need for our meeting.

This sentence implies that there is more than one file. Without the *that* clause, the reader would not know which file the writer meant. Thus, the *that* clause is essential.

Note: In choosing between *which* and *that* for beginning a modifying expression, you should always use *which* when the phrase or clause is nonessential and *that* when the phrase or clause is essential:

Nonessential: Go find Gwen, *who knows the answer,* and ask her to come too.

This sentence construction implies that there is only one Gwen. The *who* clause adds information about Gwen but does not define her. Thus, the *who* clause is nonessential.

Essential: Go find someone *who knows the answer* and ask that person to come too.

The *who* clause says which *someone* the reader must find. The reader must find only someone who knows the answer. Thus, the *who* clause is essential.

See section 412c, page 76, for more information on setting off common interrupting clauses. See also section 901, page 232, for more discussion of clauses beginning with *that/which/who/whose*.

Some transitional expressions, including *that is, namely,* and *for example*, are frequently used to *introduce* nonessential phrases or clauses. In this case, both the transitional expression and the nonessential phrase or clause are set off with commas:

> The seminar also offers recreational activities, *for example, swimming, rowing, and aerobics,* at no extra cost.

> He called himself a "bit-head," *that is, someone who knows a lot about computers,* and did not seem to mind the label.

> I need one thing, *namely, a window view,* to have the perfect office.

With Dates and Addresses | 415

When used in sentences, the separate elements of addresses and dates are set off by commas, as shown below:

> He lives at 11 Canyon Road, Denver, CO 87325, during the winter months.

> She lived at 1823 Nakomis Avenue, LaCrosse, until she was a teenager.

> Our president was born on July 4, 1925, in Florida. [See Note, page 78.]

> The conference will begin on Monday, March 5, 1994, at the Hilton in Boston.

> Let's get together again in August 1995 to discuss your financial plans. [No comma is needed between month and year or after year when no day is given.]

Let's get together on March 9, 1991 (I think I'll be ready by then). [*Note:* The comma is omitted after the year if another punctuation mark is required, in this case a parenthesis.]

Note: Although not recommended, omitting the comma after the year is becoming increasingly acceptable:

Our plane leaves on Saturday, July 14, 1993 for Holland.

See section 602, page 148, for information on the foreign/military style of writing dates.

| 416 | **With Personal and Company Names and Titles** |

Follow the guidelines below:

a. Professional Position or Educational Degree. Use commas to set off titles that refer to a person's professional position or educational degree:

Robin Boyers, *M.D.*, is hosting an open house in honor of the clinic's grand opening.

Our company just delivered a huge order to Robert Hilger, *Ph.D.*, our newest customer.

Other examples: CPA, DDS, Ed.D., M.A., M.S.

See Part 7: Abbreviations for information on using periods with abbreviations. See section 703, page 164, for more information on using and abbreviating academic, professional, and religious designations.

b. Personal and Company Abbreviations. Generally, do not set off personal and company abbreviations (and other designations) that are considered part of the person's and company's names (see Note following examples):

Randall Dupree *Jr.* holds office hours today.

Last year we celebrated the retirement of Randall Dupree *Sr.*

Lynn Anderson *III* will leave early today to attend his grandfather's 90th birthday party.

Rilex *Inc.* just signed the contract.

Gonzales *Ltd.* has expanded its sales territory to include the entire West Coast.

Note: Some people and companies prefer to have these abbreviations set off. Signatures, letterheads, telephone directories, and coworkers may help you determine individual preferences.

See sections 702, page 162, and 704b, page 167, for more information on personal and company name abbreviations.

Commas That Separate Sentence Elements

With Introductory Elements 417

Generally, use a comma to separate an introductory word, phrase, or dependent clause from the rest of the sentence:

a. Single-Word Transitions. Generally, use a comma to separate single-word transitional expressions that begin sentences:

Therefore, I will ask you to join our committee.

Furthermore, we cannot afford to advertise there.

However, I will consider it.

Nevertheless, let's include selling stock as a possibility.

Thus, we must look forward to this year cautiously.

However, you may omit the comma, if you prefer. The lack of a comma tends to deemphasize the introductory word:

> *Thus* he proceeded to work on the computer after reading the installation information.

Note: When a transitional word or a parenthetical word functions differently (i.e., not as a transition or as an aside), separating it with a comma from the rest of the sentence is usually an error:

> *However* he decides to do it, I will agree. [In this sentence, *However* functions as an adverb and means "in whatever way."]

> *Obviously* he wanted to go to the convention since his project was being used as a model of efficiency. [In this sentence, *Obviously* functions as an adverb that is important to the meaning of the sentence. It is not an aside of the writer's opinion.]

See section 435, page 104, for information on using these words with the semicolon.

Note: Do not use a comma to separate most single-word adverbs that begin a sentence:

> *Tomorrow* I will get to work early.

> *Certainly* I will go if no one else can.

> *Recently* she began an evening course on spreadsheet management.

> *There* you will find what you need.

> *Unfortunately* she could not join us.

b. Phrases and Dependent Clauses. Use a comma after introductory phrases and dependent clauses:

To get there from here, turn south on Third Street. [Phrase]

Eating lunch at her desk, she got mustard on the report. [Phrase]

Rather than taking Denise and Roger, take John. [Phrase]

When you go, tell her I'll be a little late. [Clause]

If you cannot be at the meeting, please send someone to take notes. [Clause]

What he wants this time, I cannot imagine. [Clause]

Why they want to make this change, I'll never understand. [Clause]

Note: You may omit commas after very short introductory phrases (not dependent clauses) as long as the sentence meaning is clear:

In the past I have helped on Saturdays.

During the meeting he took several pages of notes.

See section 417e, page 87, for handling introductory phrases and clauses when normal subject-verb word order is changed. See section 423, page 95, on using commas to prevent confusion.

Some words that typically begin introductory phrases and dependent clauses are:

after	between	to
although	by	under
as	during	unless
at	if	until
because	in	when
because of	on	whenever
before	over	while

behind	since	with
besides	through	without

c. Phrases and Dependent Clauses after the Main Clause.
When a phrase comes at the end of the main clause, or when a
dependent clause follows the main clause, do not separate the
phrase or dependent clause from the main clause:

You will find another ream of paper *in the back of the
cupboard*. [Phrase]

He likes *to get to work early*. [Phrase]

He tried to help *because he felt sorry for them*. [Clause]

Please send someone to take notes *if you cannot be at the
meeting*. [Clause]

See section 417b, page 84, for information on using commas
with introductory phrases and dependent clauses.

d. Phrases or Dependent Clauses as Subjects. Phrases
or dependent clauses that serve as the subject of a sentence are
essential elements; they are not introductory. Do not separate
such phrases and clauses from the rest of the sentence:

Running for public office would interfere with my personal
life. [Phrase]

To park in the president's spot is a mistake. [Phrase]

That the company must be sold is no longer in doubt. [Clause]

What my insurance company needs is proof of the accident.
[Clause]

See section 308, page 40, for information on phrases and
clauses used as subjects of sentences.

e. Normal Word Order Changed. Sometimes a sentence's normal word order is reversed so the subject follows the verb (or part of the verb). Introductory phrases and dependent clauses used in such sentences are usually not separated from the rest of the sentence by a comma:

introductory clause   v   s   v
Only after she returns the report can I present the findings.

Sentences with Two or More Main Clauses	418

When connecting two or more main clauses, follow the guidelines below:

a. Comma and Conjunction. Use a comma with the appropriate conjunction to separate the clauses of a sentence containing two main clauses. Note in the examples below the seven conjunctions used for this purpose: *but, and, or, yet, so* (meaning *therefore*), *for* (meaning *because*), and *nor*:

We hired two new assistants, *but* I kept my old office.

You take the Mann case, *and* I will take the Morris case.

Call me and let me know, *or* I will pick you up at 7:00.

She asked me to work late, *yet* she planned to leave early herself.

He told me to call, *so* I will find a telephone at the airport.

He left early, *for* he was tired and still had two stops to make.

I have not eaten today, *nor* do I intend to eat.

I like McElroy a lot, I have just met Guitterez, *and* I don't know Leisz. [Three main clauses are connected following the rules for connecting items in a series. *See section 419, page 89.*]

Note: To remember these seven conjunctions, use the acronym FANBOYS (*for, and, nor, but, or, yet, so*).

Note: Omitting the comma when connecting very short main clauses is generally acceptable:

> You go or I will.

> He came so I left.

Note: Many of the conjunctions discussed in this section also connect words and phrases. When these conjunctions connect words and phrases, do not use commas:

Wrong:	She works for Roberta, and Ron.
Rewrite:	She works for Roberta and Ron.
Wrong:	She said I could have Friday, or Monday off.
Rewrite:	She said I could have Friday or Monday off.
Wrong:	Will you work in the accounting department, or the production department?
Rewrite:	Will you work in the accounting department or the production department?
Wrong:	Jeffers wanted the window office, but accepted the middle office gracefully.
Rewrite:	Jeffers wanted the window office but accepted the middle office gracefully.
Wrong:	His work was slow, but accurate.
Rewrite:	His work was slow but accurate.

See section 413, page 77, on contrasting expressions for exceptions to this rule.

b. Comma Alone. Do not connect two or more main clauses with a comma while omitting the conjunction. This error is called a *comma splice* and results in a *run-on sentence*:

Wrong: He read the letter aloud, she took notes.

Rewrite: He read the letter aloud, *and* she took notes.

or

He read the letter aloud; she took notes. [A semicolon can be used to separate two main clauses without a connecting conjunction. *See section 433, page 103.*]

See section 419a below for information on connecting three main clauses with commas and a conjunction. See section 427, page 97, for connecting two full sentences with a colon.

Three or More Items in a Series | 419

Follow the guidelines below:

a. Commas between Items in a Series.   Use commas between the items in a series of three or more similar items. Note that the items may be single words, phrases, or clauses:

I'll be working *Mondays, Wednesdays, and Fridays* this year. [Three words in a series.]

Taking meeting minutes, using the copying machine, and keying documents are my favorite job duties. [Three phrases in a series.]

She sent her assistant *to the basement, to the supply cabinet, and to the vice president's office.* [Three phrases in a series.]

Mel looked *behind his desk, under the file cabinet, and on top of the shelves.* [Three phrases in a series.]

We're looking for someone *who knows desktop publishing, who has used a computer network, and who can manage the office if necessary.* [Three clauses in a series.]

I have never done it, I did not do it today, and I will not do it tomorrow! [Three clauses in a series.]

Note: When expressing a company name that includes a series, write it as the company writes it. If you cannot determine how the company writes its name, follow the standard rule above for punctuating items in a series:

Wilson, Smith, Moon, and Hebert, Attorneys

See section 436, page 105, for information on using semicolons to separate items in a series.

b. No Comma When Conjunctions Are Present. Do not use commas if each item is separated from the next by a conjunction, such as *and* or *or*:

I need *pencils and paper and paper clips* for my desk.

Give me *some coffee or an aspirin or an early lunch.*

| 420 | **Series of Adjectives** |

When using a series of two or more adjectives, follow these guidelines:

a. Two or More Adjectives Modifying the Same Noun. Use commas to separate the adjectives:

This time let's hire a *productive, efficient* assistant.

Please find the *large, red* folder in the file.

We waited a *long, long* time.

b. One or More of the Adjectives and the Noun Functioning as a Unit. When the adjective just preceding the noun functions together with the noun as a unit, omit the comma between that adjective and the one before it. A good test is whether the word *and* can replace the comma. If so, then a comma is appropriate; if not, omit the comma:

Wrong: She was a capable, ambitious, medical assistant. [*Medical assistant* functions as a unit. *Capable* and *ambitious* describe the medical assistant.]

Rewrite: She was a capable, ambitious medical assistant.

Wrong: We've had a good, fiscal year.

Rewrite: We've had a good fiscal year. [*Fiscal year* functions as a unit. *Good* describes that unit.]

c. Adjective Following the Noun. When two adjectives follow the noun they modify, separate them with a conjunction (usually *and*) instead of a comma. When more than two follow the noun, punctuate them as you would any series. Note that the group of adjectives as a whole is set off by commas because it interrupts the main flow of the sentence:

The new office, *spacious and plush,* was too expensive for me.

The manager's report, *concise, well researched,* and *clearly written*, explained the company's new benefits plan.

See section 414, page 77, on setting off nonessential modifiers.

Nonessential Elements   421

Use a comma to separate nonessential modifiers and other nonessential sentence elements that are placed at the end of the sentence:

a. Words. At times, single-word transitions or insertions of the writer's opinion appear at the end of a sentence. When they do, separate them from the rest of the sentence with a comma:

Let's wait until next week to discuss that, *however*.

The company's earnings declined sharply, *unfortunately*.

See section 412a, page 74, for a discussion of single-word interrupters.

b. Phrases. Nonessential phrases often end sentences. When they do, separate these phrases from the rest of the sentence with a comma:

I should hire three new workers, *including an assistant and a receptionist*.

I like word processing, desktop publishing, and accounting, *to name a few*.

I must have a copy of those minutes, *by the way*.

Jacques was a great assistant, *to tell the truth*.

Randy and Wilma must be included, *of course*.

I need two assistants on this project, *not three*.

The seminar also offers recreational activities, *for example, swimming, rowing, and aerobics*.

Note: Sentence-ending phrases that are essential modifiers should not be separated from the rest of the sentence:

Can you find labels *such as those on Nancy's desk*? [The *such as* phrase defines *which* labels and, therefore, is essential.]

The word *like* often replaces *such as* to begin essential modifying phrases:

Can you find labels *like* those on Nancy's desk?

See sections 412a–c, pages 74–76, for further discussion of interrupting phrases. See section 414b, page 78, for further discussion of essential and nonessential phrases. See section 413, page 77, for a discussion of contrasting expressions.

c. Clauses. Nonessential clauses often end sentences. When they do, separate these clauses from the rest of the sentence with a comma:

He was the best manager we had, *as I see it.*

When Frank was hired, he was the only man in the department, *I believe.*

She will promote her on Monday, *or so I was told.*

His vacation is coming up soon, *which is lucky.*

The purchasing department has hired seven new employees, *some of whom will also report to the sales manager.*

See section 412c, page 76, for further discussion of interrupting clauses. See section 414c, page 80, for further discussion of essential and nonessential clauses.

Separations To Avoid	422

Some writers use commas incorrectly to separate sentence elements that should not be separated. Avoid using commas in the situations described below:

a. Separating Subject and Verb. Do not separate a subject from its verb with a single comma:

Wrong: The *reason* she gave me for going, *is* that she wants to learn about database management.

Rewrite: The *reason* she gave me for going *is* that she wants to learn about database management.

Note: A *pair* of commas sets off a nonessential element that is placed between a subject and its verb:

> The *reason* she gave me for going, to be honest, *is* that she wants to learn about database management.

See section 412, page 74, for more information on setting off interrupting elements.

b. Separating Adjective and Noun. Generally, do not use a comma to separate an adjective from the noun it modifies:

Wrong: We all worked some long, *productive, hours* this weekend.

Rewrite: We all worked some long, *productive hours* this weekend.

See section 420, page 90, for other rules governing the use of commas with adjectives.

c. Separating a Conjunction and the Word That Follows. Generally, when a conjunction connects two clauses, do not separate the conjunction from the word that follows it:

Wrong: She passed the test, *and,* she took the job.

                        or

             She passed the test *and,* she took the job.

Rewrite: She passed the test, *and* she took the job.

Wrong: She passed the test *because,* she studied hard.

Rewrite: She passed the test *because* she studied hard.

See sections 417c, page 86, and 418, page 87, for information on punctuating a dependent clause that follows the main clause and on connecting two or more main clauses with a comma and a conjunction.

However, when a transitional conjunction begins the sentence or begins the second of two main clauses, a comma usually follows the conjunction:

Therefore, let's not discuss this issue again.

I looked everywhere for the file; *however,* she found it right on top of my desk.

See sections 412a, page 74, and 435, page 104, for more information on punctuation with transitional conjunctions.

Commas Used To Clarify

To Prevent Confusion	423

Sometimes commas are necessary to help clarify a sentence for the reader:

Unclear: After Bill Brady will go.

Rewrite: After Bill, Brady will go.

Unclear: In survey 12 29 is the average.

Rewrite: In survey 12, 29 is the average.

Unclear: Soon after the meeting began to break up.

Rewrite: Soon after, the meeting began to break up.

See section 417, page 83, for more information on punctuating introductory elements.

424 | In Place of Repeated Words

When words or phrases are repeated in similarly structured phrases and clauses, you can sometimes omit words without losing clarity. Indicate this omission with a comma:

Those going to our new branch should take Highway 11, and those going to our old branch, Seventh Avenue. [The comma between *branch* and *Seventh Avenue* indicates that the phrase *should take* has been omitted.]

425 | With Common Expressions

Some standard "sayings" need a single comma to mark the break between what would be two independent clauses if the expressions were completely written out:

First come, first served. [This means, "Those who come first will be served first."]

Garbage in, garbage out. [Usually used in reference to computers, this means, "If you put bad information in, you will get bad information back."]

APOSTROPHE

426 | In Contractions

Use an apostrophe to indicate where a letter or letters (or number or numbers) are missing in contractions:

Full Word or Phrase	Contraction
cannot	can't
he is	he's
should not	shouldn't
would have	would've

we are	we're
it is	it's
the 1990s	the '90s

Note: Do not use contractions in very formal writing, such as formal reports.

Apostrophe Spacing. Do not space before or after an apostrophe appearing within a word. When an apostrophe appears at the beginning or the end of a word, treat the apostrophe as the first or last letter of that word, and space accordingly.

See section 812, page 189, for information on forming plurals of alphabet letters, numbers, and abbreviatons. See sections 813–819, pages 190–193, for information on forming possessives.

COLON

To Introduce a Full Sentence 427

Use a colon between two sentences if the first sentence introduces the second and the second sentence makes the main point:

She asked me an important question: Will the new budget be ready by the end of the month?

The company president cited his reasons for denying the loan: The repayment period was too long, and the interest rate was too high.

See section 432, page 102, for rules concerning capitalization after colons and more information on colons introducing full sentences. See sections 433-435, pages 103-105, for information on connecting two or more full sentences with semicolons. See section 442, page 112, for information on using colons with quotation marks.

428 | To Introduce Lists

A colon is often used within or at the end of full or partial sentences to introduce lists:

a. Lists within a Sentence. Use a colon after a main clause to introduce a run-in list (that is, a list within a sentence). Do not capitalize the items in the list, but punctuate them as you would a series of items in a sentence (*see section 439, page 109, for punctuation rule*):

> I promised my employees three things: fairness, honesty, and effectiveness.

Do not use a colon after a verb or a preposition introducing a run-in list that completes the sentence:

Wrong: My assistant received an award for: efficiency, productivity, and leadership.

Rewrite: My assistant received an award for efficiency, productivity, and leadership.

Wrong: My committee members are: Roger Anderson, Lee Sung, and Rachel Geiger.

Rewrite: My committee members are Roger Anderson, Lee Sung, and Rachel Geiger.

Note: When an expression such as *for example, namely,* or *such as* introduces a series, you need not use a colon before the expression since the expression serves the same purpose (introducing) as the colon. However, a colon may be included if you prefer:

Our new manager has several good qualities: *for example,* a fair, honest attitude, compassion, and a sense of humor.

or

Our new manager has several good qualities, *for example,* a fair, honest attitude, compassion, and a sense of humor.

b. Vertical Lists. Use a colon to introduce a vertical list that is separate from a full or partial introductory sentence. Do not separate the listed items from each other with punctuation. Also, if listed items are numbered, lettered, or designated by some other symbol, capitalize the first letter of each listed item:

We have two goals today:

1. To determine the issues in question
2. To propose program changes

My reasons for agreeing with this proposal are:

a. It will increase company profits.
b. It will increase shareholder profits.
c. It will improve conditions for workers.

The three types of people who tend to shop here are:

■ Sports and fitness enthusiasts
■ Health-food eaters
■ Nutritionists

See section 403, page 69, for information on punctuating within vertical lists.

However, when creating vertical lists of single words or creating lists of more than one column, you need not designate the listed items with numbers, letters, or other symbols. Also, you need not capitalize the first letter of each listed item:

I promised my employees three things:

> fairness
> honesty
> quality

The lottery winners at the company picnic were:

8469	8467	8743
9257	8788	0033
0485	9000	5645
2930	0257	3210
8401	0981	9543
8653	1278	6556

Note: When using a colon to introduce a vertical list, make sure that the sentence immediately preceding the list is the actual introduction to that list:

Wrong: The following three steps are used in writing any business correspondence. Make sure you use them:

1. Planning information and organization
2. Writing the first draft
3. Revising to a finished document

The first sentence in the example, which refers to *the following three steps*, actually introduces the list. *Make sure you use them* incorrectly comes between the introduction and the list.

Rewrite: Make sure you use the following three steps when writing any business communication:

1. Planning information and organization
2. Writing the first draft
3. Revising to a finished document

To Express Time, Proportion, and Ratio | 429 |

Use colons to express time, proportion, and ratio. Note that no space appears on either side of these colons:

Time: 8:45 a.m.

Proportion and Ratio: 2:1

See section 601, page 147, for information on time expressions. See section 605, page 150, for information on mathematical expressions.

With Letter Salutations | 430 |

Use colons after salutations in formal letters and business letters:

Dear Ms. Williger:

See section 1008, page 270, for more information on salutations in business letters.

With Titles | 431 |

Many books, articles, speeches, and other reference sources have both a title and a subtitle. When it is necessary to write the full title, use a colon to separate the title and subtitle:

Writing between the Lines: A Guide to Subtle Persuasion

Slash and Burn: How To Cut the Deadwood from Your Writing

Note: If the author already uses some other punctuation mark between the title and subtitle, use the author's punctuation instead of the colon:

Thinking Critically in the Office—Solving Business Problems without the Policy Manual or the Reference Guide

See section 442, page 112, for information on using colons with quotation marks. See section 439, page 109, for information on using quotation marks with titles. See section 450, page 121, for information on underlining and italicizing with titles.

| 432 | **Capitalization after a Colon** |

Capitalize the word following a colon in the following cases:

a. Colon before Proper Noun or Adjective. If the word following a colon is a proper noun or adjective, capitalize it:

He spoke three languages: English, French, and German.

See section 502, page 133, for information on proper nouns and adjectives.

b. Colon after a Heading. If the colon follows a short introductory element that functions as a heading, capitalize the first letter of the information following the colon:

Note: Use only the specially purchased fax paper in the fax machine.

c. Colon Introducing the Main-Idea Clause. If the material following the colon is a main clause that expresses the main idea of the entire sentence, capitalize the first letter of that main clause:

I have only this to say: We cannot allow Hochsteder and Company to outsell us this year.

d. Colon Introducing Two or More Full Sentences.   If the material following the colon consists of two or more full sentences, capitalize the first word of each sentence following the colon:

I know of two delays: First, the finance committee has not yet approved the budget. Second, the new program manager has not yet been hired.

e. Colon Introducing Full-Sentence Quotation.   If the material following the colon is a full sentence or more quoted from another source, capitalize the first letter of each quoted sentence:

Snodgrass said this about college: "It is there that thinking is truly possible in a way that it might not be possible somewhere else."

See section 501c, page 131, for capitalization in vertical lists.

SEMICOLON

Most good writers use semicolons sparingly. Often, you can improve a complicated sentence that contains semicolons by editing the sentence to use some other punctuation mark.

To Connect Sentences without Conjunctions | 433 |

Use a semicolon (without a conjunction such as *and*, *but*, and *or*) to join two or more closely related sentences:

Her keyboarding skills were second to none; she was asked to work on any project whose deadline was approaching.

Finding the Anderson Inc. file is never easy; three managers are currently working with this company.

Petry planned the project; Willard implemented the project; Watts evaluated the project.

See section 418a, page 87, for use of conjunctions and a comma to connect two or more main clauses. See section 442, page 112, for information on using semicolons with quotation marks.

Semicolon Spacing. Insert one space after a semicolon and no space before.

| 434 | **To Connect Sentences with Conjunctions** |

You may use a semicolon instead of a comma when the joined sentences are especially long or complex or when one or both sentences already contain commas:

> Ms. Whitting arrived last night, I am told; but because her plane was late, she could not attend the opening of the leadership conference.

| 435 | **To Connect Clauses with Transitional Words or Phrases** |

Certain transitional words and phrases are often used with semicolons to connect two main clauses. Examples of these words and phrases are:

accordingly	nevertheless
consequently	otherwise
for example	that is
furthermore	therefore
however	thus
moreover	

When these transitional words and phrases connect two main clauses, the transitional words usually follow the semicolon and are followed by a comma:

> She applied for the promotion to the vice president's office; *however*, Mark Richards was promoted instead.

Equipment has been reported missing from several offices; *therefore,* security will be increased, and only one exit will be available on weekends.

Note: Do not use a semicolon with these transitional words or phrases unless they connect two *complete* clauses:

Wrong: He got up late and; therefore,was late for work.

Rewrite: He got up late and, therefore, was late for work.

Wrong: She decided to improve her meeting skills; that is, listen more carefully, take better notes, and speak up when she has an opinion.

Rewrite: She decided to improve her meeting skills, that is, listen more carefully, take better notes, and speak up when she has an opinion.

See section 412, page 74, for information on setting off with commas transitional expressions that interrupt sentences.

To Separate Items in Series   436

Use semicolons (instead of commas) to separate items in a series of three or more items that already contain commas:

My best sales occur each year in Madison, Wisconsin; Des Moines, Iowa; and Topeka, Kansas.

We are sending the following people to this year's conference: Ms. Rudolf, Director of Farming Studies; Mr. Willis, Coordinator of Agricultural Programs; and Ms. Casey-Bryant, a manager trainee.

Note: If the series contains only two items, the semicolon is unnecessary:

My best sales occur each year in Madison, Wisconsin, and Des Moines, Iowa.

See section 415, page 81, for commas separating elements in addresses and dates. See section 419, page 89, for information on using commas to separate items in a series.

QUOTATION MARKS

Tech Tip

On most typewriters and many word processing programs, the same key is used to provide both the beginning (left) and ending (right) quotation mark. However, with some word processing programs and most desktop publishing systems, different characters are available for the beginning and ending quotation marks. Use the separate characters for the left and right quotation marks when available.

437 | To Quote the Words of a Speaker or Writer

When quoting your own or someone else's words, follow these guidelines:

a. Exact Words Spoken or Written by Someone Else.
Use quotation marks to indicate that the words within are the exact words spoken or written by someone else:

She asked, "What time should I be here in the morning?"

When I asked him for a raise, he said, "I'll consider it."

"Being in business is like being in a race."

"I must say," he added, "that you have all been great."

"Without you," the chairperson said, "our committee will be at a loss. But we will struggle on."

"We must not hesitate," warned Mr. Row. "The competition will not allow it."

The chairperson said: "Without you our committee will be at a loss. We will simply have to struggle on." [When a quotation continues to a second sentence, use one set of quotation marks to contain the entire quotation.]

See sections 440–445, pages 110–117, for information on using and spacing quotation marks with other punctuation.

b. Partial Quotation of Another's Words. When you quote only part of a speaker's or writer's sentence, do not set off or separate the quotation with commas:

"An excellent meeting" is what Rachel called it.

Rachel called it "an excellent meeting."

Rachel said that the "excellent meeting" lasted a little too long.

Note: Follow standard capitalization rules when quoted material fits into the natural sequence of the sentence, as in the examples above.

c. Indirect Quotations. Do not use quotation marks with indirect quotations:

Direct Quotation: She said, "I am leaving." [The writer uses the speaker's exact words.]

Indirect Quotation: She said that she was leaving. [The writer reports what the speaker said. The writer changes word and word order to refer to the speaker.]

Wrong: He said that, "Being in business is like being in a race."

Rewrite: He said that being in business is like being in a race. [Indirect quotation.]

or

He said, "Being in business is like being in a race."
[Direct quotation.]

Wrong:	She asked, "What time she should be here in the morning."
Rewrite:	She asked what time she should be here in the morning. [Indirect quotation.]

or

She asked, "What time should I be here in the morning?" [Direct quotation.]

d. Your Own Words. Use quotation marks to indicate exact, direct statements you have spoken *aloud* in the past or intend to speak aloud in the future:

And so I said to him, "Get out!"

Whenever she asks me for advice, I will tell her, "Sorry, I have nothing to say."

However, your *written* thoughts, opinions, and questions are not considered direct quotations:

Wrong:	My question is this: "When will our raises come through?"
Rewrite:	My question is this: When will our raises come through?

Quotation Mark Spacing. Insert no spaces between quotation marks and the characters that come immediately within.

---

438 | To Draw Attention to Words and Phrases

Quotation marks are sometimes used to draw attention to words and phrases. For example, a writer may use slang, cliches, or language that is purposely incorrect or informal:

His was a real "fly-by-night" business. [*Fly-by-night* is informal; it is also a cliche.]

I'm sorry, Bob, but I "ain't gonna" do it. [*Ain't gonna* is incorrect language, which the writer probably used to lighten his refusal to Bob.]

If we cannot hold the meeting on Thursday, Friday will be our "rain day." [A *rain day* is an alternate day in case the meeting cannot be held on the day originally planned. *Rain day* is informal.]

To Indicate Titles

Use quotation marks to indicate titles of short literary works (e.g., short stories and poems), articles, songs, essays, and so on. Also use quotation marks to indicate titles of parts of longer works, such as, chapters of a book or sections of a long report:

Believe it or not, I base my career philosophy on a poem titled "April Inventory."

Tuesday I read a good article, "How To Manage Your Career."

Words from America featured the essay "America's Business and Future." [*Words from America* is a full-length work and is, therefore, italicized (*see section 450, page 121*). *"America's Business Future" is part of that work and is, therefore, set in quotation marks.*]

I especially like that book's third chapter, "Managing Your Time for Success."

Note: Standard book parts such as the preface, the appendix, the table of contents, and so on, are not placed in quotation marks.

See section 503b, page 141, for information on capitalizing major words in titles.

When quoted material contains other quoted material or titles, use single quotation marks within regular quotation marks:

> Dan said, "If you sing 'Yankee Doodle' one more time, I will never come to another party of yours."

> Gunter asked, "What did you say when Mr. Howard said, 'I want you to be at work this weekend'?"

> Gavin said, "All three of us have just finished reading 'Creating a Creative Business Environment.' " [Note that both the single and double quotation marks are placed outside the period. Also, there is a space between the single and double quotation marks.]

Note: If a single quotation mark key is not available on a typewriter or word processor, use the apostrophe key.

Place periods and commas inside ending quotation marks:

> Gavin said, "All three of us have just finished reading 'Creating a Creative Business Environment.' "

> When George recited "The Pledge of Allegiance," Mr. Dillworthy said, "We should do this at the beginning of every meeting."

> Let's collect the index cards and create a manual "database."

> "You had better find the supply room," said Al.

Quotation Mark Spacing. When you use periods and commas within quotation marks, do not insert spaces between the punctuation mark and the quotation mark. Space once after a comma used to help introduce the quotation.

a. Comma with Full-Sentence Quotation within a Sentence. When a full-sentence quotation is part of another full sentence, use a comma instead of a period to end the full-sentence quote:

"This report is too long," Mr. Merkins complained.

See also section 443b, page 114, for using a question mark or exclamation point instead of the comma.

b. Comma To Set Off Nonessential Quotations. When placing a quotation within a sentence, use commas to set off the quotation if it is a nonessential sentence element:

My favorite song, "Blue Moon of Kentucky," was a hit before I was born.

His closing remark, "Women have no business on this committee," ended the speech on a ridiculous note.

See also section 414, page 77, on using commas to set off nonessential modifiers.

c. Commas To Set Off Interruptions in Quoted Material. When you interrupt a single quotation within a sentence, use two sets of quotation marks, one for each part of the quotation. Also, set off the interrupting element by commas:

"I must say," he added, "that you have all been great."

d. No Commas To Set Off Essential Quotation. When placing a quotation within a sentence, do not use commas to set off the quotation if it is an essential sentence element:

Say "Please hold while I ring his office" when transferring a call to Mr. Long.

The article "How Any Business Can Improve" should be read by our management team.

Place colons and semicolons outside quotation marks:

> Rosalyn said it best: "It's simple. We must outproduce and outsell our competition to stay in business."

> There are three things we must improve "with all speed": hiring, training, and motivating.

> He was not just "one of the team"; he was our only hope of writing a good grant by the deadline.

Colon and Semicolon Spacing. Insert no space between the colon or semicolon and the quotation mark. When quotation marks follow colons or semicolons, space as you normally would after colons (*see Tech Tip, page 98*) and semicolons (*see section 433, page 103*).

a. Colon Instead of Comma. When a full sentence introduces the quotation, use a colon instead of a comma after the introductory sentence:

> The committee's report concluded only this: "We can no longer meet until the budget committee has developed its plan."

See also section 432e, page 103, for more information on colons introducing quotations.

b. Colon To Introduce Long Quotations. When the quoted material is two or more sentences or is separate from its introduction, use a colon to introduce the quoted material:

> Our president said: "I must commend the budget committee for all its efforts. Our budget is sound, our departments are up and running with plenty of financial resources, and our budget process is still intact."

Our president said:

> I must commend the budget committee for all of
> its efforts. Our budget is sound, our departments
> are up and running with plenty of financial
> resources, and our budget process is still intact.

Note: When a quotation requires three or more lines on the
written or keyed page, separate and indent the quotation as in
the second example above. Do not use quotation marks with
separate, indented quotations; the indentation and introductory
sentence identify the material as a quotation.

Question Marks and Exclamation Points with Quotation Marks   443

Placing question marks and exclamation points inside or outside
quotation marks depends on whether the quotation marks
contain the full question or exclamation or only part of the
question or exclamation. Follow the guidelines below:

**a. Quoted Question or Exclamation Ending the
Sentence.** If the quoted material contains the entire question
or exclamation, place these punctuation marks inside the ending
quotation mark:

The visitor asked, "How can I find the manager's office?"

Gloria said, "I demand to see him now!"

When quoted material ends a sentence, a second
end-punctuation mark is usually not used. When you must
choose, use exclamation points rather than periods, and use
question marks rather than exclamation points or periods:

Wrong: Did the visitor ask, "How can I find the manager's
             office?"?

Rewrite: Did the visitor ask, "How can I find the manager's
             office?"

Wrong:	I cannot believe she said, "I demand to see him now!"!
Rewrite:	I cannot believe she said, "I demand to see him now!"

However, when using quotation marks to enclose a title that ends with an exclamation point or question mark, include both end-punctuation marks:

Are you going to attend the seminar "Manage It!"?

I loved the seminar "Manage It!"!

Are you reading the article "How about Telecommuting?"?

I loved the movie "What about Telecommuting?"!

Also, when an abbreviation ends a sentence that also ends with quoted material, use both the period attached to the abbreviation and the sentence's end punctuation when the end punctuation is not a period:

My friend asked Ms. LaRue, "Are you getting your Ph.D.?"

Are you sure he said, "She will arrive at 8:00 a.m."?

He said, "She will arrive at 8:00 a.m." [End the sentence with only one period.]

b. Quoted Question or Exclamation Beginning or within the Sentence. If the quoted material contains the entire question or exclamation, place these punctuation marks inside the ending quotation mark. Note that the question mark and exclamation point replace the comma that would appear if the quoted material were not a question or exclamation:

"Is this report too long?" Mr. Merkins asked.

He asked, "Do you have any messages for me?" and kept walking right out the door.

"This report is too long!" Mr. Merkins complained.

Earl shouted, "Not today!" and slammed the door.

c. Quoted Material as Part of Question or Exclamation. If the quoted material is only part of the question or exclamation, place these punctuation marks outside the ending quotation mark:

When did she say, "Have two keys made"?

Have you ever heard Pachebel's "Canon"?

When you said, "You're fired," what did you mean?

She would not stand during "The Star Spangled Banner"!

See section 443a, page 113, for more information on using end-punctuation marks with quotation marks. See sections 407–408, pages 71–72, for information on using question marks. See section 410, page 73, for information on using exclamation points.

Exclamation Mark and Question Mark Spacing. Insert no space between these two punctuation marks and the quotation marks.

Parentheses with Quotation Marks	444

If quoted material is part of a parenthetical element, make sure both quotation marks are inside the parentheses. If an element in parentheses is part of the quoted material, make sure both parentheses are inside the quotation marks:

I cannot find my favorite story ("When I Grow Up").

"I am a member of WBVA (a professional organization)," she said proudly.

Spacing with Parentheses: Insert no space between a parenthesis and a quotation mark.

See sections 448–449, page 119, for information on using parentheses.

<table>
<tr><td>445</td><td>**Other Punctuation with Quotation Marks**</td></tr>
</table>

a. Ellipsis Mark for Omissions. When words are left out of quoted material, insert an ellipsis mark (three spaced periods) to indicate this omission to the reader. Although the ellipsis mark consists of spaced periods, do not space between the ellipsis mark and other punctuation marks:

"In the middle of the day . . ., workers often need a short break," the expert explained. [No space between the ellipsis marks and the comma.]

"If given the choice, most workers . . . would choose recognition over money," Wilson added.

"What will you do when you retire . . .?" she asked the audience.

Ms. Winslow said: "Take your papers down to the library. Go to the reference desk, and ask for the annual report. . . . This will answer your question." [The ellipsis mark after the period indicates that one or more full sentences were omitted from the quotation.]

The report stated:

. . . a second problem is lack of motivation. Workers in the mail office spend little time each day interacting with workers from other departments . . . . In addition, the lack of natural lighting in the basement will, over time, lead to a lack of energy. [The first ellipsis mark indicates that this quotation began in the middle of the original sentence. The second ellipsis mark indicates that something was omitted at the end of the second sentence.]

Note: The material that remains after an omission must leave the sentence sounding complete. Also, the omission does not affect standard punctuation rules, including commas and end punctuation.

b. Brackets for Additions. When you must insert something in quoted material for clarity or to add information, use brackets:

"When I return to the office [from vacation], I will find what you need," she said.

Note: If you cannot use brackets, use parentheses.

DASH

Dashes replace other punctuation marks, most often commas, parentheses, colons, and semicolons. Use dashes sparingly, especially in formal writing, because another punctuation mark is almost always preferred.

To Introduce or Summarize Information   446

Dashes are often used in informal writing to introduce or summarize information:

I'll need some supplies to get me started—some black and blue pens, a pad or two of paper, and a calendar.

Germany, Czechoslovakia, Bulgaria, Poland—all these formerly communist countries are now open to the West.

Dash Spacing. Insert no space between the dash and the characters that come before and after it.

With most typewriters and many word processing systems, a dash is formed by connecting two hyphens. However, some word processing programs and most desktop publishing systems allow you to create a full dash, or *em dash* (the width of the letter *m*), without connecting hyphens. Of course, these same systems also allow you to key an *en dash* (the width of the letter *n*) to indicate a range as in 1990–1995.

To Set Off or Separate Information 447

Dashes may be used instead of commas or parentheses to set off or separate sentence elements from the rest of the sentence. Setting off or separating information with dashes tends to emphasize that information:

Please send the meeting notice to Kent, Audre, Rita—and, of course, Marilyn.

Her discussion of business opportunities in Germany, her hints on new business grants—and especially her introduction to the European Economic Community—were all helpful.

Please call Jorge—find his number in my book—and ask him to attend Wednesday's meeting also. [Full sentences set off by dashes within other sentences do not begin with a capital letter or end with standard end punctuation.]

See sections 412, page 74, and 449, page 119, for information on using commas and parentheses to set off interrupting elements.

PARENTHESES

Parentheses usually indicate information that serves as an aside, that is, information that is additional but nonessential to the sentence or paragraph.

Use parentheses to enclose sentences or groups of sentences offering additional or explanatory information that is not essential to the message of the paragraph:

> Two days ago, Ms. Couret and I met with representatives from our Anglo-French Relations Committee. The committee recommended that we consider two sites for our new European headquarters: Paris and Marseilles. *(The committee noted that Calais was too far from the economic center of France.)* Please study the detailed notes attached, along with my summary of the advantages and disadvantages of each site, and be prepared to discuss these options at our July meeting.

Note: When complete sentences are placed in parentheses and are not within other sentences, standard sentence capitalization and punctuation rules apply.

Spacing with Parentheses. Insert no spaces between either parenthesis and the character immediately within it. Spacing after the final parenthesis depends on the function of the parentheses:

1. If parentheses set off a full sentence within a paragraph, space after the final parenthesis as you would after a period.

2. If parentheses are used within a sentence, e.g., *(see section b below)*, use a single space between the final parenthesis and the next word, and do not space between a final parenthesis and another punctuation mark.

Use parentheses to indicate nonessential elements within a sentence. Placing information within parentheses tends to deemphasize that information:

> Please send one case of white (not brown) envelopes.

Please deliver the Stanwick report on Friday (by 1:00, please) so our committee chair can have a copy to review over the weekend.

We have two Lincolns on the lot (one red, one black) and several Oldsmobiles.

We have only one Model 354 left (they are selling very well right now) but a dozen or so Model 349s. [The first word of the material in parentheses is not capitalized even though it begins a full sentence. The only exceptions are proper nouns, the pronoun I, or quoted material that is already capitalized.]

Earlier, I mentioned that I would arrive by plane (see my letter of June 8), but I have decided to drive.

Elsewhere in this report (see page 47) you will find a list of the cities we are targeting this year.

In her final year in office (1990), she pushed that bill through the committee.

Our first president, Herbert Welchell (1912–1978), left this company in solid financial condition. [When referring to important people, their birth and death dates are often enclosed in parentheses.]

The party we are planning (can you come?) is being moved to Apartment 78A.

Note: When parentheses are placed within a sentence, make sure they do not include some word or punctuation mark that is essential to the rest of the sentence:

Wrong: If the vice president calls (her assistant's name is Richard,) let her know that I will be a few minutes late for the budget meeting.

Rewrite: If the vice president calls (her assistant's name is Richard), let her know that I will be a few minutes late for the budget meeting.

See section 414, page 77, for discussion of essential and nonessential sentence elements.

UNDERLINE AND ITALICS

Underlines or italics can be used to indicate titles, to emphasize sentence elements, to set off words being discussed, and to indicate foreign words or phrases.

> When you use a typewriter, underlining may be your only option for punctuating in the situations described below. However, users of word processing and desktop publishing systems usually have the better option available: italicizing.
>
> *Tech Tip*

To Indicate Titles
450

A common use for underlining or italicizing is to indicate titles of books, magazines, newspapers, and full-length literary, artistic, or written works:

A coworker reminded me that *Gone with the Wind* was really about economics.

Consumer Reports is the favorite magazine of many shoppers.

Twin Cities Magazine is gaining popularity with local businesses. [*Magazine* is included in the underlining and capitalized because it is part of the title.]

Time magazine features a business section each week. [The word *magazine* is not part of the title and, therefore, is not underlined or capitalized.]

Note: Punctuation and possessive endings that are not part of a title are not included in the underlining or italicizing of that title. Punctuation marks that are part of the title should be included:

The book *What's a Business To Do?* was on the best seller list last week.

Whenever I read *Newsweek*, I am impressed by the reporting.

Whenever I read *Newsweek*'s reporting, I am impressed.

See section 439, page 109, for information on using quotation marks to indicate titles.

| 451 | **To Emphasize** |

Underline or italicize to emphasize a sentence element:

I could not *believe* she said that!

Should we really be taking *that* to the conference?

Note: If you underline or italicize too often, the emphasizing effect will be lost. Be selective.

See section 438, page 108, for information on using quotation marks to draw attention to words and phrases.

| 452 | **To Mark Words That Are Discussed as Words** |

At times, you will discuss words in your written communication. When doing so, underline or italicize the word that is the topic of discussion:

I don't think the word *monumental* is too strong.

Are you sure *promotion* is the right word here?

Courageous is too long. Try *brave.*

We take *manage* to mean "creating an environment in which work is completed accurately and efficiently." [The word being discussed is underlined or italicized, and the definition is quoted.]

Note: Some writers use quotation marks instead of underlining or italicizing when marking words discussed as words.

To Indicate Foreign Words or Phrases 453

Avoid using foreign words or expressions in your writing, unless you can find no English alternatives. If you must use foreign words and phrases, underline or italicize them (see Note below examples):

To that I must say, "*Au contraire!*" [Better sentence: I disagree with that.]

Are long breaks *verboten*? [Better sentence: Are long breaks forbidden?]

Note: If you find a foreign term, expression, or abbreviation in an English dictionary, assume it has become standard English usage and do not underline or italicize it. Examples are:

ad hoc	etc.
status quo	et al.
vice versa	ibid.

See Part 7: Abbreviations for more information on abbreviations.

HYPHEN

Hyphens are commonly used to form compound adjectives, nouns, and verbs. In these cases, hyphens help readers understand that a combination of words has a single meaning and function in the sentence, as in the phrase *state-of-the-art machines*. Hyphens are also used occasionally to connect prefixes to root words, especially when an unhyphenated spelling may confuse the reader.

Using hyphens to create compounds can be complicated because so many variables are involved and because the construction of a compound may change as it becomes widely used. For these reasons, you should always consult a current dictionary when you question the spelling of a compound word. (In most cases, the spellings in this section follow those in *Webster's Ninth New Collegiate Dictionary*.) When you cannot find the word you need in your dictionary, follow the guidelines below.

| 454 | **With Compound Adjectives** |

A compound adjective results when two or more words function together as one to modify a noun or pronoun. Use a hyphen to connect the words that form a compound adjective:

The bank gave us a *30-year* mortgage. [The adjective *30-year* modifies *mortgage*.]

Follow the *easy-to-read* instructions. [*Easy-to-read* modifies *instructions*.]

That plan is not *cost-effective*. [*Cost-effective* modifies *plan*.]

She is a *high-ranking* member of our committee. [*High-ranking* modifies *member*.]

Our problem is *two-sided*. [*Two-sided* modifies *problem*.]

We can't offer those *unheard-of* prices! [*Unheard-of* modifies *prices*.]

Avoid *run-on* sentences in your letters. [*Run-on* modifies *sentences*.]

Take advantage of the *on-the-job* training. [*On-the-job* modifies *training*.]

We attended the *quality-management* seminar. [*Quality-management* modifies *seminar*.]

However, when the above compound adjectives (and similar compounds) no longer function as a single modifier, do not hyphenate them. For example:

The instructions are *easy to read*.

The seminar on *quality management* offered helpful information.

She received excellent training *on the job*.

Note: Though some style manuals recommend it, there is no need to hyphenate adverb-adjective combinations because the grammatical construction makes the meaning clear. The adverb modifies the adjective, and the adjective modifies the noun:

He is a *well known* attorney. [The adverb *well* modifies the adjective *known*.]

She supplied the *much needed* leadership. [The adverb *much* modifies the adjective *needed*.]

The *newly formed* committee will handle employee complaints. [The adverb *newly* modifies the adjective *formed*.]

With Compound Nouns 455

A compound noun results when two or more words function together to form a single noun. A compound noun may be written as one word (*airmail, database, layout*), as two words (*word processing, problem solving, decision making*), or as a hyphenated construction (*sit-in, close-up*). How compound nouns are written often indicates their prevalence in our language. Well established compound nouns often appear as single words while new compound nouns appear as two words or with a hyphen.

Compound nouns written as single words and many common two-word and hyphenated compound nouns usually appear in a dictionary. Check your dictionary for the correct spelling. If your dictionary does not include the compound noun you want, use a hyphen to connect the words that form the compound:

The employees held a *sit-in* to protest working conditions.

We will use a *stand-in* for the *close-ups*.

What a *time-saver* this date book has been!

The president had a *falling-out* with the CEO.

We must consider all the *trade-offs*.

We're having a *get-together* after work tomorrow.

However, when the above word combinations (and other hyphenated compound nouns) function as a different part of speech and no longer as a unit, do not hyphenate them. For example:

The students will *sit in* the president's office until she listens to their complaints. [*Sit* functions as a verb, and *in* functions as a preposition.]

Let's *get together* after work for a dinner meeting. [*Get* functions as a verb, and *together* functions as an adverb.]

See section 807, page 188, for information on forming the plural of compound nouns. See section 815, page 191, for information on forming the possessive of compound nouns.

456 | With Compound Verbs

A compound verb forms when two or more words function together as a single verb. Common compound verbs are often written as single words: *brainstorm, download, proofread, troubleshoot*. Check a dictionary for the correct spelling. If your dictionary does not list the verb, use a hyphen to connect the words that form a compound verb:

Anita will *pinch-hit* for the president while he is gone.

The cooks will *deep-fry* or broil the fish right at our tables.

Double-space the report and make eight copies.

Note: Do not hyphenate verb-adverb constructions:

I'll *follow up* on that proposal.

We can't *turn down* that offer unless we have good reasons.

The network decided to *black out* the game.

| 457 | **With Prefixes** |

Most common prefix-root combinations appear in the dictionary; check your dictionary for any word in question. For prefix-root combinations not listed, write the word without a hyphen:

nontraditional	antiestablishment
preestablished	micromanager
reemphasize	cooperate
ultrabasic	biweekly

Note that your dictionary will include some exceptions, for example:

anti-intellectual
co-op (short for the noun *cooperative*)

Also, when a common word containing a prefix is used with a less common meaning, use a hyphen between the prefix and the root to avoid confusion. For example:

Common	***Less Common***
I'll help you *recover* from your operation.	I'll help you *re-cover* your sofa.

Let's not *resort* to
bidding too low on the
project.

To locate the letters from
new clients, Alison will
re-sort the mail.

Note: Do not confuse the hyphen with the dash (*see sections 446 and 447, pages 117 and 118*).

See sections 822–831, pages 195–198, for information on using hyphens to divide words at the ends of lines of typed text. See section 602, page 148, for information on using hyphens to punctuate ranges of numbers. See section 605d, page 151, for examples of using hyphens to express common fractions as words.

CAPITALIZATION
- To Indicate a New Sentence
- To Indicate a Proper Noun
- To Indicate Titles

PART FIVE

NOTES

CAPITALIZATION

To Indicate a New Sentence 501

Always capitalize the first word of a new sentence. In addition, capitalize in the following situations:

a. First Word of a Full-Sentence Quotation. Capitalize the first word of a full-sentence quotation:

He said, "Bring that file here, please."

See also section 437, page 106.

b. First Word of an Independent Question within a Sentence. Capitalize the first word of an independent or full-sentence question within another sentence except when the full-sentence question is set off by dashes or parentheses:

The question is: When may I see my personnel file?

The new seminar schedule (did you receive a copy?) does not include the motivational program.

See sections 447, page 118, and 449, page 119, for exceptions to this rule when setting off a full sentence with dashes.

c. First Word in a Vertical List. Capitalize the first word in each listed item when the listed items are designated by letters, numbers, or other symbols. Capitalize even if the listed items are introduced by only a partial sentence and the listed items are not full sentences:

When you come to the meeting, please bring:

    a. The computer printout of current budget spending
    b. The file on Binghamton Companies
    c. Any contracts needing signatures

If you go tomorrow, please remember the following:

1. Harold will meet you at the hotel.
2. The meeting begins at 6:30.
3. I'll look for a fax from you tomorrow evening.

See sections 403 (page 69), 404 (page 70), and 428b (page 99) for more information on vertical lists. See section 432, page 102, for other situations in which capital letters are used after colons.

d. First Words in Outline Sections. Capitalize first words in sections of formal outlines:

PRESENTATION OUTLINE

I. Introduction

II. Project history

   A. Before Simmons began

      1. Undefined goals

      2. Poor planning

      3. Unmanageable process

   B. After Simmons began

      1. Returned to planning stage

      2. Simplified process

      3. Oversaw process carefully

III. Goals for next phase of project

See section 1034, page 306, for more information on preparing and formatting outlines. See section 402, page 68, on using periods in outlines.

e. Letter Salutations and Complimentary Closings.
Capitalize each word in a salutation but only the first word
in a closing:

Salutation: Dear Personnel Director:

Closing: Sincerely yours,

See sections 1008, page 270, and 1011, page 273, for more
information on salutations and complimentary closings in
business letters.

To Indicate a Proper Noun	502

Common nouns name classes or groups of people, places, and
things. Proper nouns refer to specific people, places, or things
by their official names. Proper nouns always begin with a
capital letter. The following table lists some common nouns
together with an example of an official name (proper noun)
within that group:

Common Nouns	*Proper Nouns*
president	Abraham Lincoln
building	Sears Tower
mountain	Mount Everest
river	Mississippi River
book	*Rabbit Is Rich*
play	*Death of a Salesman*
historical event	Louisiana Purchase
copier	Xerox® copier
doctor	Doctor Guiterrez

company	Honeywell Corporation
	The Times Inc.
organization	Boy Scouts of America
award	the Nobel Prize

Note: Minor words such as prepositions, articles, and conjunctions are not capitalized unless the name is printed that way by the particular company or organization.

See section 307, page 39, for information on potential subject-verb agreement problems when proper nouns function as subjects. See section 503b, page 141, for information on capitalizing only major words in titles.

a. Proper Adjectives. Sometimes proper adjectives are formed from proper nouns. Most proper adjectives should be capitalized the way their corresponding proper nouns are capitalized:

American	Roman
English	Arabic
Japanese	Greek
Columbian	Asian

Sometimes a proper adjective is used with a common (uncapitalized) noun:

Harvard graduate

Rhodes scholar

Note: Check your dictionary if you cannot determine whether a word or phrase is common or proper.

b. Personal Names. Just as you would spell a person's name as that person does, punctuate and capitalize the name as that person does also. For many names, several possibilities exist:

Steven VanDame Jr.

Steven van Dame Jr.

Stephen Van Dame, Jr.

Steve van Dame, Jr.

See section 416b, page 82, for information on using commas with personal titles such as *Jr.* See sections 809–810, pages 188–189, for information on forming the plural of proper names.

c. Place Names. Capitalize geographical place names:

Dallas

Texas

the state of Texas

Kansas City

the city of Topeka

Note: Capitalize *city* only when it is part of the actual name. This is also true of words such as *state, upper, lower,* and *the.*

Also, capitalize alternative or fanciful names for geographical places:

the Big Apple (New York City)

the Windy City (Chicago)

the Coast (usually the West Coast)

the Beaver State (Oregon)

the Sun Belt (area of United States)

the State (when replacing specific name
that is obvious in context)

d. Directional Names. Capitalize the names of directions only when they refer to major geographical regions (or a person from that region). Do not capitalize directional names when they merely indicate direction or describe a geographical feature such as coast, plains, or ridge:

I'm going to the *East Coast* this winter. [Name of a region.]

President Powell recently visited the *Middle East*. [Name of a part of the world.]

Fishing is great in the *Midwest*. [Name of the central region of the U.S.]

The *Southeast* has a lot of textile manufacturing. [Name of a U.S. region.]

George Marshall claimed to be a *Southerner*. [Proper name given to a resident of a particular region.]

We'll travel to *Northern* Ireland for the seminar. [*Northern* is part of the country's name.]

but

I'm going *east* on Highway I-94. [Indicates direction.]

The *eastern coast* of the United States borders the Atlantic. [Describes a geographical feature.]

President Indira recently traveled *west*. [Indicates direction.]

Fishing is great just *south* of here. [Indicates direction.]

To the *southeast* is a textile manufacturing plant. [Indicates direction.]

We'll travel to *southern* Florida for the conference. [Not an official region name, but a general descriptive term.]

See section 705, page 167, for information on abbreviating compass points.

e. Time Periods. Capitalize names referring to specific time periods:

Common Nouns	*Proper Nouns*
day	Wednesday, Saturday
month	February, November
holiday	Memorial Day, Fourth of July
historical period	Middle Ages, Bronze Age
historical decade	the Roaring Twenties

f. Government Acts. Capitalize major words in the official names of government acts and legislation:

the First Amendment

the Civil Rights Act of 1965

Prohibition

Public Law 667

the Warsaw Pact

the Treaty of Versailles

g. Races, Peoples, Languages, Religions. Capitalize the official names of races, peoples, languages, religions, and supreme beings:

English	Asian
Chinese	Hmong
Hispanic	Buddhist
Native American	Muslim (or Moslem)
African American	Roman Catholic
Latin	Jewish
Greek	God

Note: The terms *blacks* and *whites* (or *black* and *white*) when used to refer to African American and Caucasian people are usually not capitalized.

h. Number and Letter Designations. Capitalize words that precede or are designated by numbers or letters only when those designations are complete, official titles or labels. When the designations are partial or when they identify common or generic locations, do not capitalize them:

Examples using complete official titles or labels:

He finally made it to *Grade 6* on the pay scale.

Refer to *Appendix B*: *Sales History* for more information.

You will find that in *Part III* of *Volume II* of the report.

I'm looking for *Purchase Order 1479-B* and *Invoice 84573*.

Let's meet in *Room 816*, just down the hall.

Examples using partial or common titles or labels:

Looking at *figure 4-2*, you can see in *column 2* of *row 12* how our profits rose in December. [*Figure 4-2* has a complete title that includes a description of the graph. *Column 2* and *row 12* are simply generic identifications of a position on a table.]

I found no mention of it in *diagram C* or *illustration 1.4*. [Both the diagram and the illustration have complete titles that identify their contents.]

Look at *lesson 4* of *chapter 10*, for example. [Both the lesson and the chapter have longer official titles.]

Take a look at *line 7* of *paragraph 2* on *page 43*. [All three simply describe generic locations that occur in many documents.]

See section 604, page 149, for information on using figures to label numbered objects. See Part 6: Numbers for information on using figures and words to express numbers in sentences.

i. Hyphenated Terms. Capitalize only those parts of hyphenated terms that are proper nouns or adjectives:

Please send *French-speaking* interpreters.

We must have our *mid-January* budget report ready by the end of the week!

At the inaugural party, *President-elect Thompson* spoke nervously.

Note: When hyphenated words or phrases function as capitalized headings, in a report or newsletter, for example, each word of the phrase should begin with a capital letter:

In Sentence	*As Heading*
French-speaking interpreters	French-Speaking Interpreters
mid-January budget report	Mid-January Budget Report

See sections 454–456, pages 124–126, for information on using hyphens to form compound adjectives, nouns, and verbs.

To Indicate Titles | 503

Capitalize official, occupational, family, and literary titles as described below:

a. Official Titles. Capitalize official titles when they immediately *precede* the person's name in a sentence and serve as an official title rather than a generic job title:

Last week President Jones asked to adjourn early.

I learned this from ex-President Adler. [Notice that the prefix *ex-* is not capitalized. This is also true of words such as *late* and *elect* when they modify titles.]

but

Jones is our president.

Last week Jones, our president, asked to adjourn early.

Last week our president, Jones, asked to adjourn early.

However, the titles of high-ranking national and international officials and dignitaries should be capitalized when they *follow* the person's name, when they *replace* the person's name, and when they *precede* the person's name. High rank is defined as follows:

International: People known worldwide, such as the Pope, the Secretary General of the United Nations, and the Queen of England.

National: Top-level officials in the U.S. government, such as the President, the Vice President, cabinet officials, members of Congress, and heads of government agencies; also top-level national officials from other countries, for example, Prime Minister:

> The President of the United States will meet with his cabinet members to discuss an emergency situation.

> Elizabeth II, Queen of England, visited the Canadian provinces last month.

> Who will be named Ambassador to Ireland?

When similar titles designate local or state officials, you need not capitalize them. However, to be consistent, you may choose to capitalize these local and state titles, along with others, such as:

the Mayor

the Governor

the Representative

b. Major Words in Official Titles. Capitalize major words, which include nouns, pronouns, adjectives, adverbs, and verbs. Do not capitalize prepositions (e.g., *of, for, to, with, on*), conjunctions (e.g., *and, but, or*), or articles (i.e., *the, a, an*). Some reference sources recommend capitalizing longer prepositions such as *between, among, within, through*, and so on. Doing so, however, leads to inconsistent capitalization and is not recommended.

c. Government Bodies and Official Organizations. Capitalize major words in names of government bodies and official organizations:

the United Nations

the Bush Administration

the United States Congress

the Food and Drug Administration

the California State Department of Education

the New York State Legislature

the University of Georgia

the Press Club of America

Alcoholics Anonymous

the United Auto Workers of America

Boys and Girls Clubs of America

the Huntsville Church of Christ

See section 503b above for information on capitalizing only major words in titles.

d. Occupational and Family Titles. Generally, do not capitalize occupational or family titles such as manager, assistant, accountant, father, and mother, unless those titles appear in direct address. In direct address, the title usually replaces someone's name:

This is our new *assistant*, Lisa Welch.

Linda Davis is *office manager* now.

Robin is now *senior accountant*.

I'll ask my *father* whether he can join us.

Can you join us, *Father*? [Direct address.]

Would you explain this to me once more, *Professor*? [Direct address.]

I need to know, *Mother*, when you will be taking vacation. [Direct address.]

e. Department and Committee Names. Capitalize the names of departments and committees only when they are the official names of the unit. If they are simply descriptive titles, do not capitalize them:

Our *Accounting Department* has lost all computer power for the next three hours. [*Accounting Department* is the official name of the department.]

Our *production department* is behind schedule. [The official name of the department is *Development and Production Department*.]

Do not capitalize such titles when they do not refer to a specific situation but are discussed more generally:

Many companies spend a lot of money in their *production departments*.

Every *credit department* runs a little differently.

See section 503b, page 141, for information on capitalizing only major words in titles.

f. Titles of Written or Performed Works. Capitalize the first word and all major words in titles of written or performed works:

Death of a Salesman

"The Annual Report of the Hightower Financial Corporation"

"How To Succeed in Life or Business" [Capitalize the word *To* when it is used with a verb in an infinitive phrase.]

"Moving between a Rock and a Hard Place: Corporate Career Ladders" [*See also section 431, page 101, for examples of capitalizing after colons in titles.*]

"Moving Up the Corporate Ladder: Ten Suggestions" [Although prepositions should not be capitalized in titles, words such as *up, on, down, off,* and others should be capitalized when they function as adverbs. *See section 321, page 62, for more information on the distinction between adverbs and prepositions.*]

See section 503b, page 141, for information on capitalizing only major words in titles. See sections 439, page 109, and 450, page 121, for information on using quotation marks, underlining, and italicizing to indicate titles.

g. Academic Courses. Capitalize major words of the titles of academic courses. Do not capitalize general areas of study. Also do not capitalize academic degrees unless they are used as titles (usually abbreviated) attached to people's names:

You should definitely take *History 201.*

You should definitely study *history.*

All students took *history, English,* and *math.* [*English* is capitalized because it is the name of a language; *see section 502g, page 137.*]

I earned an *associate's degree* last fall while she finished her *doctoral degree.*

She is now Phyllis Wheats, *Ph.D.*

NOTES

NUMBERS

- Time Expressions
- Dates and Decades
- Money
- Numbered Objects
- Measurement and Mathematical Expressions
- Numbers with Symbols and Abbreviations
- Numbers Expressed as Words
- Numbers Modifying Numbers
- Numbers in Legal Documents

NOTES

NUMBERS

Numbers are written in figures or words, depending on the situation. In general, use figures to express all numbers in technical writing and to express physical measurements, money, and time in nontechnical writing. When consistency allows, use words for the numbers one through ten and for particular situations as illustrated in sections 608 and 609.

Time Expressions $\boxed{601}$

Use figures to express clock time:

Pick me up at *4 a.m.* so I get to the airport on time.

Pick me up at *4:30 a.m.* so I get to the airport on time. My plane leaves at *4:56 a.m.*

Let's meet at *8 o'clock* tonight. [Generally, use phrases such as *in the evening* or *in the afternoon* with *o'clock* Also, time designations of *p.m.* and *a.m.* are preferred over *o'clock.*]

When writing 12:00, use *midnight* or *noon* rather than *12:00 a.m.* or *12:00 p.m.* Readers may not be sure which abbreviation refers to midnight and which refers to noon:

We open for deliveries at *midnight.*

Let's meet at *noon.*

Use *morning, afternoon, evening*, or *night* when specific clock times are not present. Use *a.m.* and *p.m.* only with numbers. Do not use both *morning* and *a.m.*, for example, since the two expressions mean the same:

Let's talk to Frank *next Thursday afternoon.*

but

Let's talk to Frank *next Thursday at 3:15 p.m.* [Not *at 3:15 p.m. in the afternoon.*]

See sections 706 (page 170), 707 (page 171), and 709 (page 174) for information on time-related abbreviations.

| 602 | **Dates and Decades** |

Use figures to express dates and decades:

The new quarter begins on April 1.

On September 1, 1992, we began our fourth year.

We began in September 1989.

By the 1990s, we should show a profit.

The '80s were not good years in our business.

From 1985 to 1987, our management received record bonuses.

Have your budget plans ready by March 10, 1995. [See Note below on military and international dates.]

Our best years were 1985–1989. [See Note immediately below.]

Note: Hyphenate number ranges that do not use a *from-to* construction (if an en dash is available with your software, use it instead of a hyphen):

Our best years were *1985–1989.*

but

Our best years were *from 1985 to 1989.*

Note: Correspondence from military and international organizations will often reverse the day and month in dates, as shown below. Use this method if it is the practice of the organization to which you are writing:

Have budget plans ready by *10 March 1995*.

See section 415, page 81, for information on using commas in dates. See section 426, page 96, for information on using apostrophes in contractions. See section 812, page 189, for information on using apostrophes for number plurals.

Money	603

Use figures to express amounts of money:

I did not have enough cash for the *$4* tip.

Take the *$4.00* out of Anderson's envelope.

Mr. Antonio did not have enough cash for the *$22.75* bill or even the *$4.00* tip. (*See section 607f, page 156, on consistent number expression.*)

Please provide *$17.50* out of the petty cash fund.

I wouldn't give *50 cents* for that copier today!

See section 609, page 157, for information on using numbers in legal documents.

Numbered Objects	604

Use figures to number and label specific objects:

Look at *number 3* on the list, for example.

Figure 9 illustrates my point.

How are sales in *Region 5*?

See section 502h, page 138, for rules concerning capitalization of numbered objects.

| 605 | **Measurement and Mathematical Expressions** |

Use figures for measurements and other mathematical expressions:

a. Measurements. Use figures to express numbers in measurements:

The flooring needed is for an office *8 feet by 10 feet*.

The flooring needed is for an office *8 x 10 feet*.

The flooring needed is for an office 8′ x 10′. [*See sections 708–709, pages 172–174, for information on abbreviating units of measurement and on expressing dimensions.*]

We will need an *8- by 10-foot* piece of carpet. [*Use hyphens to indicate compound adjectives. See section 454, page 124.*]

Tell me whether the package weighs more than *1 pound 8 ounces*. [There is no comma between the pounds and ounces since the entire phrase appears as one element.]

Even a letter of *1 ounce* requires a first-class stamp.

When the thermometer dips to *10 degrees*, I stay home.

b. Decimals. Use figures to express decimals:

He measured the desk at *5.5 feet*.

The square root of 10 is *3.1622776*.

Sales were up only *0.95* percent from last year. [Use the zero before the decimal point to prevent misreading.]

c. Percentages. Use figures to express percentages. Use the word *percent* or the % symbol consistently within a document:

I'll ask for a *10 percent* raise.

We noticed an *8%* increase in employee absences.

She received a *6.5 percent* raise. [Use decimals instead of fractions whenever possible because they are easier to read.]

d. Fractions and Mixed Numbers. Generally, use figures to express fractions and mixed numbers in technical writing or in reference to physical measurements:

The next step will require an 11/32 drill bit.

We need another 3-1/2 feet of cable.

We need another *3-1/2* feet of cable. [When fractions are available on your keyboard, do not space or hyphenate between whole number and fraction. Also, if you must use fractions *not* supplied on the keyboard, form all fractions the same way, using the diagonal mark (/).]

If the fraction appears alone without the item it refers to or does not express a direct physical measurement, spell out the fraction:

May I work *two-thirds* time for *two-thirds* salary?

He makes only *half* of what I make.

I can't answer *one-half* the questions she can answer.

More than *a quarter* of my pay goes to taxes.

The president announced that *nine-tenths* of the profits were reinvested in the company.

She won the election by a *two-thirds* majority.

See section 454, page 124, for information on using hyphens to form compound adjectives.

606 | Numbers with Symbols and Abbreviations

Use figures to express numbers with symbols and abbreviations:

| $5 | 7% | 9 in. | 9" | fig. 6 | p. 2 | No. 1 |

See Part 7: Abbreviations for more information on abbreviations. See section 710, page 180, for more information on symbols.

607 | Numbers Expressed as Words

Use words to express numbers in the following situations:

a. Numbers One through Ten. Generally, use words to express numbers one through ten as long as consistent number expression is maintained:

We now have *ten* committee members to edit this report.

Please find *seven* volunteers and *one* company van.

but

Juan ordered *12* dozen pencils and *4* dozen pens. [Use the same form—figure or word—to express numbers used similarly within a sentence. If one of the numbers is above 10, use figures for both numbers.]

See sections 601–606, pages 147–152, for exceptions to this rule. See section 607f, page 156, for information on consistent number expression.

b. Beginning of Sentence. Do not begin a sentence with a figure. Instead, spell out the number or rearrange the sentence to maintain consistent number expression throughout a document:

Wrong:	47 people attended the meeting.
Rewrite:	Forty-seven people attended the meeting.
Wrong:	100 people came to the meeting.
Rewrite:	There were 100 people at the meeting.

or

One hundred people came to the meeting.

Wrong:	1992 was his retirement date.
Rewrite:	He retired in 1992.

c. Indefinite Numbers. Spell out indefinite numerical expressions in which words such as *several, many,* and *few* function as part of the number:

Several hundred people have expressed their interest. [*Several* is part of the indefinite number.]

but

About 600 people have expressed their interest.

Many thousands of customers opted for our rebate. [*Many* is part of the indefinite number.]

but

Nearly 4,000 people opted for our rebate.

A few million square miles of ocean could be polluted by our oil spill. [*A few* is part of the indefinite number.]

but

About 2 million square miles of ocean could be polluted by our oil spill. (*See section 607d below, for information on using figures to express extremely large numbers.*)

d. Extremely Large Numbers. Readers will more quickly comprehend large numbers that are spelled out; therefore, spell out the thousands and millions parts of extremely large, rounded numbers as shown below:

That market would allow us to reach about *11 million* customers.

The world has more than *5.4 billion* people. [Express fractions contained in large numbers by their decimal equivalents. Common fractions such as one-half or one-quarter may also be spelled out.]

Use figures or words as shown below to maintain consistency of number expression within a document (*see section 607f, page 156):*

We now sell to over *one* million customers nationally.

or

We now sell to over *1* million customers nationally.

However, when you must express large, unrounded numbers precisely, use figures:

Our database shows *1,029,934* customers, to be exact.

We had *1,029,934* customers last year and this year hope to have *2,000,000*. [Use the same form for all related numbers in a sentence or document.]

Note: To help readers quickly interpret large numbers, use commas (without spacing) to separate each set of three digits within numbers:

1,000

42,467

1,000,000

26,043,802

5,002,465,009

Tech Tip Do not use commas in numbers when you enter numbers in databases and spreadsheets. Most database and spreadsheet programs do not accept commas during the entry process. Also, many database and spreadsheet programs will automatically format numbers according to program defaults.

e. Ordinal Numbers. In general, express ordinal numbers as words:

Who was the *first* to arrive?

He was the *fifth* assistant we hired this year.

They celebrate their *fifteenth* anniversary this month.

Next year will be our *twenty-fifth* year in business.

Our founder celebrates her *forty-third* birthday today.

But if the ordinal number becomes more than two words when spelled out, use figures:

The city of Granger celebrated the *125th* anniversary of its founding.

See section 1006c, page 267, for information on using ordinal numbers in street addresses.

f. Consistent Number Expression.   When numbers designate similar things or serve similar functions within a sentence, paragraph, or document, express these numbers in similar form. Use figures rather than words if at least one number is above ten:

> If you will recruit *16* people, I can find the other *9*. [The numbers *16* and *9* both refer to *people* and are, therefore, directly related.]

> Once we have *25* people, we can move in *three* days. [The numbers *25* and *three* measure dissimilar things and, therefore, need not be expressed in similar form.]

| 608 | **Numbers Modifying Numbers** |

When a number modifies another number, spell out one of the numbers to avoid confusion:

Wrong: Our company has 15 12-story buildings in the city.

Rewrite: Our company has fifteen 12-story buildings in the city.

or

Our company has 15 twelve-story buildings in the city.

See section 454, page 124, for information on using hyphens to form compound adjectives.

In legal documents, numbers (especially dollar amounts) are expressed in both words and figures; decimals are often expressed even when the amount given is a whole number:

For the work listed above, Armex Corporation will pay a total of *Fifty Thousand Dollars ($50,000.00)*.

As agreed, we will pay *one hundred twenty-five dollars ($125.00)* for full rights to the photograph.

Note: Dollar amounts spelled out may be capitalized or not, depending on the organization's preference.

NOTES

ABBREVIATIONS AND SYMBOLS

- General Recommendations
- Personal Names
- Academic, Professional, and Religious Designations
- Organizations
- Geographic Names and Compass Points
- Days and Months
- Time
- Units of Measure
- Miscellaneous Business Abbreviations
- Symbols

PART SEVEN

NOTES

ABBREVIATIONS AND SYMBOLS

Abbreviations are selected letters (sometimes with periods) indicating a longer word or phrase: *C.P.A.* instead of *certified public accountant.* Symbols are special graphic marks that stand for a word or phrase. The dollar sign (*$*) is a commonly used symbol. When using abbreviations and symbols, follow the recommendations below:

a. When To Use. When considering whether to use abbreviations and symbols, follow this basic rule: "When in doubt, spell it out." Well known and widely used abbreviations and symbols can make your communication more efficient. But if your abbreviations and symbols confuse or frustrate the reader, you may not communicate what you intend.

Note: Do not confuse abbreviations with short forms or contractions. Except in the most formal situations, many short forms are now acceptable: *ad (advertisement), exam (examination), memo (memorandum), typo (typographical error).* Contractions use an apostrophe to indicate omitted letters: *can't (cannot), I'd (usually I would), we're (we are).*

b. Consistency. Be consistent. Form your abbreviations the same way throughout a document. Also, your decision to abbreviate is often based on your evaluation of the formality of the situation; therefore, decide before you begin writing or editing whether you will use abbreviations.

c. Introducing Abbreviations. In some situations, you will want to introduce an abbreviation your reader may not know. In this case, spell out the full word or phrase the first time it is used and follow it with the abbreviation in parentheses. After this, you may use the abbreviation, confident that your reader will understand. For example:

When I worked for the *Environmental Protection Agency (EPA)*, I found the caseload was too much to handle. At the *EPA*, one caseworker is assigned far more cases than that worker can handle effectively.

d. Abbreviation at End of Sentence. Do not add another period to end the sentence if an abbreviation with a period ends the sentence:

Pick me up at 7 a.m.

but

Can you pick me up at 7 a.m.?

You will pick me up at 7 a.m.!

Pick me up at 7 a.m.; we'll get to work early.

e. Spacing with Abbreviations. Use one space after an abbreviation in a sentence; however, do not space between an abbreviation and a punctuation mark immediately following it:

My supervisor, *Mr.* Frank, earned a *Ph.D.*, the highest academic degree possible in the United States.

| 702 | **Personal Names** |

Express a person's name as that person prefers:

J.L. Hawkins

J. Lawrence Hawkins

Jon L. Hawkins

Jon Lawrence Hawkins

a. First and Middle Initials. Include a period but no space between a person's initials. However, add a space between an initial and another part of the name:

S.J. Hawkins

S. Jack Hawkins

b. Personal Titles. Always use the following abbreviations instead of the full word form:

Singular	*Plural*
Miss	Misses
Mrs.	Mmes.
Ms.	*Mses.*
Mr.	Messrs.
Dr.	Drs.

Other abbreviations: Jr.   Sr.   Esq. (see Note below)

Note: Esq. is the abbreviation for *Esquire. Esquire* is a term rarely used today, but it does appear at times attached to lawyers' names (both male and female):

Samuel Jacobson, Esq.

Martha Worthington, Esq.

See section 901, page 223, for a discussion of *Miss/ Mrs./ Ms.* See section 416b, page 82, for information on using commas to set off *Jr.* and *Sr.* See sections 1006a, page 265, and 1012, page 273, for information on using personal or courtesy titles in business letters.

a. Attached to a Person's Name. Many abbreviations for academic, professional, and religious designations are written with periods (but no internal spacing) when attached to a person's name:

B.S.	Bachelor of Science
M.S.	Master of Science
M.A.	Master of Arts
A.S.	Associate of Science
M.B.A.	Master of Business Administration
Ph.D.	Doctor of Philosophy
R.N.	Registered Nurse
M.D.	Doctor of Medicine
Ed.D.	Doctor of Education
D.D.S.	Doctor of Dental Science

Other professional abbreviations, especially military and political abbreviations, use periods with spacing:

Gen.	Lt. Col.	Lt. Gov.
Pres.	Prof.	Sen.

Note: In formal writing, spell out these titles:

General	Lieutenant Colonel	Lieutenant Governor
President	Professor	Senator

b. As General Reference to Training or Occupation.
When used generally to designate groups of people with certain kinds of training (i.e., not attached to a person's name), these titles are often used without periods:

Michele Peak, M.B.A.	*but*	We hired two MBAs.
Mike Walsh, R.N.	*but*	This company needs a good RN on its staff.
Sarah Lithe, C.P.A.	*but*	Now we need a CPA.

Note: When using full words instead of abbreviations, express these titles in lowercase letters:

She was awarded a *bachelor of science degree.*

She was awarded a *bachelor's degree.*

He is a *registered nurse.*

c. Placement of Professional Title. When writing a person's name, use a title once, either before or after the name. Do not use two titles, even if they appear to be different:

Wrong: Dr. Delores Deirdrich, M.D.

or

Ms. Delores Deirdrich, M.D.

Rewrite: Dr. Delores Deirdrich

or

Delores Deirdrich, M.D.

Note: If you must choose between titles (e.g., Ms. or Dr.), use the one preferred by the named person. If that preference is unknown, use the professional title.

See section 416a, page 82, for information on using commas to set off academic, professional, and religious designations.

a. Specific Organizations. Abbreviated organization names are usually capitalized without periods:

AFL-CIO	American Federation of Labor and Congress of Industrial Organizations
NAACP	National Association for the Advancement of Colored People
YWCA	Young Women's Christian Association
NYSE	New York Stock Exchange
BBC	British Broadcasting Corporation
ABC	American Broadcasting Corporation
USDA	U.S. Department of Agriculture

Some organizations' abbreviations are *acronyms*. Acronyms are different from the abbreviations above only in that they are usually pronounced as full words, not letter by letter:

NATO	North Atlantic Treaty Organization
CORE	Congress of Racial Equality
WATS	Wide Area Telephone Service
TELEX	Teletypewriter Exchange
NOW	National Organization for Women
WHO	World Health Organization
HUD	[Department of] Housing and Urban Development

See section 503b, page 141, for information on capitalizing only major words in titles.

b. Standard Organization Abbreviations. Many business organizations use general, standardized abbreviations in their names. These are usually followed by a period:

Co.	Company
Corp.	Corporation
Inc.	Incorporated
Ltd.	Limited
Mfg.	Manufacturing
Mfrs.	Manufacturers

See section 416b, page 82, for information on using commas with abbreviations such as *Inc.*

Geographic Names and Compass Points	705

a. U.S. State and Possession Abbreviations. Some reference sources recommend abbreviating state names differently depending on their use. This requires additional, unnecessary memory work for business professionals; therefore, use the two-letter U.S. state abbreviations both in addresses and in text in which a street, city, and state address appears. Note that the standard two-letter abbreviations below are fully capitalized and use no internal spacing or periods:

Alabama	AL
Alaska	AK
American Samoa	AS
Arizona	AZ
Arkansas	AR
California	CA
Colorado	CO

Connecticut	CT
Delaware	DE
District of Columbia	DC
Federated States of Micronesia	FM
Florida	FL
Georgia	GA
Guam	GU
Hawaii	HI
Idaho	ID
Illinois	IL
Indiana	IN
Iowa	IA
Kansas	KS
Kentucky	KY
Louisiana	LA
Maine	ME
Marshall Islands	MH
Maryland	MD
Massachusetts	MA
Michigan	MI
Minnesota	MN
Mississippi	MS
Missouri	MO
Montana	MT
Nebraska	NE
Nevada	NV
New Hampshire	NH
New Jersey	NJ
New Mexico	NM
New York	NY
North Carolina	NC
North Dakota	ND
Northern Mariana Islands	MP
Ohio	OH
Oklahoma	OK
Oregon	OR
Palau	PW
Pennsylvania	PA
Puerto Rico	PR
Rhode Island	RI

South Carolina	SC
South Dakota	SD
Tennessee	TN
Texas	TX
Utah	UT
Vermont	VT
Virginia	VA
Virgin Islands	VI
Washington	WA
West Virginia	WV
Wisconsin	WI
Wyoming	WY

b. United States. The *United States* is often abbreviated without periods when it is part of a longer abbreviation: USAF (United States Air Force). However, when it is used by itself or when it is the only abbreviated element of an organization name, use periods but no spacing within:

U.S.

U.S. Department of Defense

c. Streets and Roads. Commonly used street, road, and thoroughfare abbreviations are:

Ave.	Avenue
St.	Street
Pl.	Place
Blvd.	Boulevard
Dr.	Drive

See appendix C for a lengthy list of abbreviations for other possible street designations. See section 1006c, page 267, for information on abbreviating consistently in street addresses.

d. Compass Points. Points of the compass in addresses may be abbreviated or spelled out, depending on space limitations and an organization's style preference. If you abbreviate compass points, also abbreviate the street designations:

> 110 Oak St. E.

> 116 W. Truman Ave.

> 3465 N.E. Beverly Dr.

When abbreviating direction and street designations for database-generated mailing labels, follow Postal Service guidelines requiring all capital letters and no periods or special punctuation:

> 110 OAK ST E

> 116 W TRUMAN AVE

> 3465 NE BEVERLY DR

When compass points appear within a sentence, but are not part of an address and do not designate a specific place, do not capitalize or abbreviate them:

> Drive *northwest* on Thomas Lane to find the office.

See section 1006c, page 267, and appendix C for information on formatting compass points consistently in addresses.

---

706 | **Days and Months**

Do not abbreviate days and months in normal text. Sometimes, however, you must use abbreviations in tables or other graphic material. In such cases, use the following three-letter abbreviations with periods:

Days		*Months*		
Sun.	Tues.	Jan.	Mar.	May
Mon.	Wed.	Feb.	Apr.	Jun.

| Thu. | Sat. | | Jul. | Sept. | Nov. |
| Fri. | | | Aug. | Oct. | Dec. |

Note: A set of shorter abbreviations may be useful, especially in graphics with limited space:

Days			*Months*		
Su	Th		Ja	My	S
M	F		F	Je	O
Tu	Sa		Mr	Jl	N
W			Ap	Au	D

See sections 707 below and 709, page 174, for other time-related abbreviations.

Time

707

Use the following abbreviations:

a.m. (also A.M.)	twelve midnight to 11:59 in the morning
p.m. (also P.M.)	twelve noon to 11:59 at night
EST	Eastern standard time
CST	Central standard time
MST	Mountain standard time
PST	Pacific standard time
DST	daylight savings time
sec.	second(s)

min.	minute(s)
hr.	hour(s)
wk.	week(s)
mo.	month(s)
yr.	year(s)

Note: When using *a.m.* and *p.m.* (or *A.M.* and *P.M.*), use the lowercase or uppercase set consistently within a document, and punctuate them correctly: periods but no spacing within. Also, note that many published materials use small capital letters to express these abbreviations.

See section 601, page 147, for information on time expressions. See sections 706, page 170, and 709, page 174, for other time-related abbreviations.

708	Units of Measure

a. U.S. Standard Units. Standard units of measure are usually abbreviated using lowercase letters with periods, without adding -*s* or -*es* to form a plural:

in.	inch(es)
yd.	yard(s)
ft.	foot (feet)
mi.	mile(s)
oz.	ounce(s)
gal.	gallon(s)
lb.	pound(s) of weight

but

mpg	miles per gallon
mph	miles per hour

Note: When these abbreviations are used as subjects, they take a singular verb. In the following sentence, for example, *4 lb.* functions as a single unit:

She says that *4 lb. is* too much.

See section 605a, page150, for information on expressing measurements. See section 708c, page 174, for information on expressing dimensions.

b. Metric Units. Metric units of measure usually have a one- or two-letter abbreviation with no period:

g	gram
l	liter [The capital L is sometimes used for clarity.]
m	meter

The following letters represent prefixes that are often combined with root words to form other units of measure. The abbreviation of a new unit is usually a two- or three-letter combination of the new prefix and root word abbreviations. For example, *2 cm* means "2 centimeters," and *2 km* means "2 kilometers."

d	deci- (prefix)
c	centi- (prefix)
m	milli- (prefix)

da	deka- or deca- (prefix)
h	hecto- (prefix)
k	kilo- (prefix)

See sections 708a, page 172, and 709 below, for abbreviations of standard U.S. units of measure and other common units of measure.

c. Expressing Dimensions. In dimensions, give simple units of measure (e.g., feet) only once:

Wrong: 8.5 ft. x 10 ft.

Rewrite: 8.5 x 10 ft.

However, when giving more complex and technical specifications, use the correct unit of measure abbreviation or symbol with each number:

8 ft. 9 in. x 12 ft. 3 in.

8′9″ x 12′3″

See section 710 , page 180, for information on symbols.

709	**Miscellaneous Business Abbreviations**

Below is a list of standard abbreviations often used in business, along with their meanings (*see section 710, page 180, for standard symbols*). Note each abbreviation's capitalization and punctuation:

acct.	account
amt.	amount
AP	accounts payable
approx.	approximately

AR	accounts receivable
ASAP	as soon as possible
Assn.	Association
assoc.	associate(s)
asst.	assistant
att.	attachment
Attn.	attention
avg.	average
bal.	balance
BL	bill of lading
bldg.	building
BS	bill of sale
ca.	approximately (often used with dates)
CAD	computer-aided design
CAM	computer-aided manufacturing
c	copy or duplicate
CD	certificate of deposit or compact disc
CEO	chief executive officer
CFO	chief financial officer
chg.	charge
CIF	cost, insurance, and freight
Co.	Company
c/o	in care of
COD	collect (or cash) on delivery
cont.	continued
COO	chief operating officer
Corp.	Corporation

CPA	Certified Public Accountant
cr.	credit
ctn.	carton
cwt.	hundredweight
dept.	department
dis.	discount
dist.	district
distr.	distributor, distributed, distribution
div.	division
DP	data processing
dr.	debit
dstn.	destination
dtd.	dated
DTP	desktop publishing
e.g.	for example
e-mail	electronic mail
EOM	end of month
enc.	enclosure
et al.	and other people
ETA	estimated time of arrival
etc.	and other things, and so on
ext.	extension (usually telephone)
FAX or fax	fascimile machine or message
FIFO	first in, first out
ft-tn	foot-ton(s)
fwd.	forward
FY	fiscal year

FYI	for your information
GM	general manager
GNP	gross national product
gr.	gross (12 dozen)
gr. wt.	gross weight
hdlg.	handling
hp	horsepower
HQ or hdqrs.	headquarters
hr.	hour(s)
I/O	input/output (computer related)
ID	identification
i.e.	that is
Inc.	Incorporated
incl.	including
ins.	insurance
intl.	international
inv.	invoice
K	kilobyte (computer capacity)
l. (ll.)	line (lines)
LAN	local area network (computer)
LIFO	last in, first out
Ltd.	Limited
max.	maximum
Mb	megabytes (computer capacity)
mdse.	merchandise
mfg.	manufacturing
mfr.	manufacturer

mgr.	manager
min.	minutes or minimum
misc.	miscellaneous
M.O.	method of operation, how something is done
mo.	month(s)
MO	mail order, money order
n/30	net in 30 days
NA	not applicable, not available
n.d.	no date
No.	number
Nos.	numbers
nt. wt.	net weight
opt.	optional
orig.	original
org.	organization
OS	out of stock
OTC	over the counter
p. (pp.)	page (pages)
P&L	profit and loss
pd.	paid
PERT	program evaluation and review technique
pkg.	package
PO	purchase order
P.O.	post office
POE	port of entry
PP	parcel post
ppd.	postage paid, prepaid

pr.	pair(s)
PR	public relations
PS or P.S.	postscript
pstg.	postage
pt.	pint or part, point(s), port
qt.	quart
R&D	research and development
RAM	random access memory (computer)
re	regarding, concerning
RFD	rural free delivery
ROM	read-only memory (computer)
RPG	report program generator
RSVP	Please respond.
qtr.	quarterly
qty.	quantity
recd.	received
reg.	registered
req.	requisition
ret.	retired
rev.	revised
rm	ream(s)
SASE	self-addressed stamped envelope
sec	second(s)
sec.	secretary
sec.	section
SO	shipping order
SOP	standard operating procedure

std.	standard
stmt.	statement
TM	trademark
treas.	treasurer, treasury
VIP	very important person
viz.	namely
vol.	volume
V.P.	vice president
vs.	versus
v.	versus (especially in legal documents)
WAN	wide area network (computer)
whsle.	wholesale
wpm	words per minute
wt.	weight
yr.	year

See sections 702–708, pages 162–174, and appendix C, or check a current dictionary for other abbreviations.

---

710 | Symbols

Except for the most common symbols (e.g., $ and %), symbols are generally used only in informal writing, in very technical material, in graphics (illustrations and charts), and in tables and schedules.

a. Spaced Symbols. When using a symbol on this list, leave a space before and after the symbol:

Symbol	*Meaning*	*Example*
@	at	2 lb. @ $1.29/lb.

&	and	Wilks & Associates
©	copyright	© 1992 by Buscom Publishing
x	by	(as in 6′x10′) 8′x10′ (8 ft. by 10 ft.)
/	per	$8/yd. ($8 per yd.)
®	trademark	Xerox® copier

Note: When the symbol & is used with capitalized initials, there is often no space between characters:

A&B Companies

See section 708c, page 174, for more information on using the symbol x to show dimension.

b. Unspaced Symbols. When using symbols on this list, leave no space between the symbol and the figure with which it appears:

Symbol	*Meaning*	*Example*
$	dollar(s)	$4.00
¢	cent(s)	50¢
°	degrees	32°
′	foot (feet)	8′ x 10′
"	inch(es)	4" x 6"
#	number (used before a figure)	#3

¶	paragraph	¶2
%	percent	10%
#	pound(s) (used after a figure)	5#
§	section	§8

See section 605c, page 151, for more information on using the % symbol.

SPELLING AND WORD DIVISION

- Plurals
- Possessives
- Division of One-Syllable Words
- Division between Syllables
- Prefixes and Suffixes
- Consecutive Line Ends
- Abbreviations, Numbers, and Contractions
- Names of People
- Dash
- Dates
- Addresses
- Word Groups That Include Numbers

PART EIGHT

NOTES

SPELLING AND WORD DIVISION

This section includes rules for forming possessives and plurals and guidelines for basic word division.

SPELLING

Lists of spelling rules exist in several reference sources, but because so many exceptions also exist, the usefulness of such lists is limited. Rather than memorizing complicated rules and exceptions, you will find it more helpful to follow three basic guidelines:

1. Use your word processor's spell checker for every document you prepare.

2. Use a dictionary for words not included in your word processor's collection or when a spell checker is unavailable.

3. Learn rules that cover word forms not always listed in the dictionary (possessives and many plurals).

> Word processing spell checkers will identify most misspellings in a document. Errors these programs cannot detect include errors in usage (you vs. your), errors in the spelling of plural and possessive word forms, and mistakes in proper nouns.
>
> *Tech Tip*

PLURALS

Basic Guideline | 801

Form the plural of most words by adding *s* to the singular form:

Singular	Plural
computer + s	computers
keyboard + s	keyboards
database + s	databases

802 Words Ending in *ss*, *ch*, *tch*, *sh*, *z*, *x*, or *zz*

Add an *es* to form the plural:

Singular	Plural
address+ es	addresses
tax+ es	taxes
approach+ es	approaches
watch+ es	watches
buzz+ es	buzzes
brush+ es	brushes

803 Words Ending in *is*

Change the *is* to *es* to form the plural:

Singular	Plural
analysis	analyses
basis	bases
crisis	crises

Nouns Ending in *y* Preceded by a Consonant 804

Change the *y* to *i* and add *es* to form the plural:

Singular	*Plural*
company	companies
industry	industries
laboratory	laboratories

Nouns Ending in *f* or *fe* 805

Change the *f* or *fe* to *v* and add *es* to make the plural:

Singular	*Plural*
half	halves
life	lives
shelf	shelves

Words Ending in *o* 806

Check your dictionary to find out whether to add an *s* or an *es* to form the plural. For some words, either form is correct:

Singular	*Plural*
fiasco	fiascos or fiascoes
veto	vetoes
tomato	tomatoes

807 | Hyphenated and Nonhyphenated Compound Words

Add *s* to the first word to form the plural:

Singular	*Plural*
letter of credit	letters of credit
father-in-law	fathers-in-law
leave of absence	leaves of absence

If there is no noun in a hyphenated compound, then add the *s* to the end of the word:

show-off	show-offs
get-together	get-togethers
spin-off	spin-offs

See section 455, page 125, for information on compound nouns.

808 | Nouns Ending in *ful*

Add an *s* to the end of the word, not to the base word, to form the plural:

Singular	*Plural*
mouthful	mouthfuls (not mouthsful)
handful	handfuls (not handsful)

809 | Basic Rule for Last Names (Surnames)

Add an *s* to form the plural:

Singular	Plural
Singular	*Plural*
Mr. and Mrs. Boitano	the Boitanos
Mr. and Mrs. Whitman	the Whitmans
Mr. and Mrs. Capote	the Capotes

Last Names That End in *s*, *x*, *ch*, *sh*, or *z* | 810 |

Add *es* to form the plural:

Singular	*Plural*
Mr. and Mrs. Jones	the Joneses
Mr. and Mrs. Fox	the Foxes
Mr. and Mrs. Metz	the Metzes

Personal (Courtesy) Titles | 811 |

See section 702b, page 163, for information on plural forms of titles such as *Mr.* and *Ms.*

Plurals of Alphabet Letters, Numbers, and Abbreviations | 812 |

Form the plurals of capital letters, numbers, and most abbreviations by adding *s* to the singular. Note, however, that if an abbreviation stands for two words (M.D. for Medical Doctor), you should add the *s* *after* the second period. But if the abbreviation stands for only one word, add the *s* *before* the period:

Singular	*Plural*
A	As
Z	Zs
chap.	chaps.

Dr.	Drs.
M.D.	M.D.s
CEO	CEOs
1990	1990s

Use an *'s* to form the plural of lowercase letters. Without the apostrophe readers may misinterpret your meaning:

Michelle spells her name with two *l's.*

There are two *s's* at the end of that name.

POSSESSIVES

Apostrophes show possession with nouns and with some pronouns. Where you place the apostrophe depends on the word's ending and on whether the word is singular or plural.

---

813 | Singular Nouns

For most singular nouns, add an *'s* to show possession:

The *manager's* desk is piled with papers.

Boston's summer celebration is a popular event.

A few singular nouns, for example, *Mr. Billings* or *Illinois,* become difficult to pronounce when you add *'s* because the addition makes an extra syllable. In this case, add only an apostrophe to show possession:

Mr. *Billings'* report   *Illinois'* capital

Note: Do not use the apostrophe simply to make a singular noun plural:

Wrong: He found two book's in the top drawer.

Rewrite: He found two books in the top drawer.

Also, do not confuse possessive forms of nouns with adjectives ending in *s*, which do not use apostrophes:

The *news* story about our company ended with a big surprise.

The *Des Moines* newspaper covered the story well.

Plural Nouns 814

Plural nouns that end in *s* require only an apostrophe:

Our company president decided to replace the *accountants'* computers.

The *deputies'* duties increased once the new captain was hired.

The personnel department tracks the *employees'* salary information.

Plural nouns that do not end in *s* require an *'s* to make them possessive:

The *women's* case was presented in court.

The conference dealt with *children's* issues.

Compound Nouns 815

To form the possessive of a compound noun, follow the basic rules for forming possessives: If the compound does not end in *s*, add *'s* to the last word. If the compound ends in *s*, add *'*:

son-in-law's birthday   *editor-in-chief's* policy

newscasters' pool   *clerk-typists'* salaries

Note: Some plural compounds may require special treatment to indicate the possessive. Many of these compounds contain "of" phrases that follow plural nouns. You can make the meaning clear by changing the entire phrase to an *of* expression:

Unclear: the boards of education's agreement

Rewrite   the agreement of the boards of education

| 816 | **To Show Joint Possession** |

To indicate that one item is owned jointly by two people, add an *'s* to the second name only:

Karen and *Bev's* office is located on the second floor. [Karen and Bev share an office.]

To indicate that each person possesses an item, add an *'s* to each name:

Karen's and *Bev's* offices are located on the second floor. [Karen and Bev each have an office on the second floor.]

| 817 | **Possessive Pronouns** |

The possessive forms of personal pronouns do not use an apostrophe:

Pronoun	*Possessive*
I	my, mine
you	your, yours

he	his
she	her, hers
it	its
we	our, ours
they	their, theirs
who (relative pronoun)	whose

However, the indefinite pronoun *one* requires an *'s* to indicate possession:

One's beliefs are the foundation of *one's* behavior.

See sections 305, page 36, and 313–317, pages 46–55, for more information on pronouns. See section 901, page 221, for information on *its/it's*.

Possessives before *–ing* Words | 818 |

When a noun or pronoun modifies a gerund (a present participle verb used as a noun), use the possessive form of the noun or pronoun:

Maria's quitting made the rest of the staff unhappy.

Do you mind *my* calling you when the books go on sale?

His working overtime brought in several new orders.

Possession with Inanimate Objects | 819 |

Traditionally, style authorities have maintained that writers should use an *of* expression with inanimate, or nonliving, things (the tines of the fork). However, using the possessive for certain inanimate nouns is becoming more widely accepted, as in:

The *company's* profits doubled last year.

The *car's* engine overheated.

I bought *50 cents'* worth of candy.

He earned a *day's* pay in two hours.

| 820 | **Time Expressions** |

The possessive of a singular unit of time is formed by adding *'s*:

one week's vacation   one month's overtime

The possessive of a plural unit of time is formed by adding only the apostrophe:

two weeks' vacation   three months' pay

| 821 | **Abbreviations** |

Follow the rules for singular and plural nouns.

Time *Inc.'s* profits   the *M.D.s'* offices

See Part 7: Abbreviations for information on common abbreviations.

WORD DIVISION

When business documents were produced only on typewriters, the rules for word division were strictly defined to achieve fairly even right margins. Now that most documents are created with word processing software, word division is usually handled automatically by the computer. However, many writers and keyboarders prefer *no* word division at the ends of lines unless they are preparing text in narrow, justified columns.

When you must divide words manually, let your dictionary guide you. Entries will indicate with dots or other marks each point at which a word may be divided. If a word is shown undivided, do not divide it.

The following guidelines, based on the 1990 printing of *Webster's Ninth New Collegiate Dictionary,* cover words not included in the dictionary and rules for the ends of paragraphs and pages.

One-Syllable Words 822

Do not divide one-syllable words even though some may be long:

| length | strengths | thoughts |

Division between Syllables 823

Divide multiple-syllable words between syllables:

| mes-sage | syl-la-ble | re-gret-ting |
| pub-lish | be-tween | per-for-mance |

Note: Although they may be correct and may appear in the dictionary, some divisions between syllables can confuse a reader, especially if one or both parts may be read as words by themselves. In such cases, break the word in a different place:

re-apportion	*not*	*reap-portion*
co-insure	*not*	coin-sure
re-educate	*not*	reed-ucate

824 | Prefixes and Suffixes

Generally, divide *after* a prefix and *before* a suffix. If the root word ends in a double consonant, divide *after* the double consonant:

bill-ing   confess-ing

When adding a suffix results in a double consonant, divide *between* the doubled letters:

commit-ting   refer-ring

825 | Consecutive Line Ends

Avoid dividing words at the ends of more than two consecutive lines within a paragraph. Also, try not to divide the last word of a paragraph or the last word on a page.

826 | Abbreviations, Numbers, and Contractions

Do not divide abbreviations, numbers in figures, or contractions:

1995 $10,000   Assoc.

didn't   approx.   No. 4

Note: Abbreviations already containing hyphens may be divided at the hyphen:

AFL-CIO   WMUS-TV   MS-DOS

827 | Names of People

Avoid dividing a person's name and avoid separating a courtesy or professional title from a name. But if it becomes essential, you may divide a first or last name according to the guidelines for dividing common words.

Dash

828

If a word is followed by a dash, do not divide before the dash or between the hyphens if your dash is created with two hyphens.

Dates

829

Date expressions at the ends of lines may be divided between the day and the year, but not between the month and the day:

April 15, 1994	*not*	April 15, 1994

Addresses

830

Do not separate the number and the street name:

9701 Washington Avenue	*not*	9701 Washington Avenue

The city, state, and ZIP Code may be divided between the city and the state or between the state and the ZIP Code:

Lincoln, NE 98765	*or*	Lincoln, NE 98765

Tech Tip

If you key a hyphenated word, for example, *self-esteem,* enter a hard hyphen to retain the hyphen between the words of the compound.

831 Word Groups That Include Numbers

Avoid dividing word groups that should be read as a unit, such as page and number, chapter and number, or number and unit of measure:

      page 311   chapter 6   29 inches

WORD USAGE
- Common Difficult Words
- Technology Terms

PART NINE

NOTES

WORD USAGE

Following are words or pairs of words, arranged alphabetically, that writers and speakers often misuse, including definitions (or synonyms) and examples of their use. In many cases, only the *most common* or *most problematic* parts of speech are given for a word, even though these words may function as other parts of speech at times. When words are given in groups or pairs, the group or pair is listed according to the word nearest the beginning of the alphabet. For an exhaustive discussion of difficult words, check your dictionary or an English usage guide.

a/an
Use *a* when the following word begins with a consonant sound; use *an* when the following word begins with a vowel sound:

a third workstation	an extra workstation
a job interview	an interview
a canceled order	an order
a reasonable boss	an understanding boss
a history book	an interesting book
a university	an hour
a unit	an honor

a lot
Write as two words: We have *a lot* of money to spend.

a while/awhile
A while: (noun) a short time period

May I use the computer for *a while*?

Awhile: (adverb) a short time

I was finished with your computer *awhile* ago.

accept/except
Accept: (verb) to take or receive

I *accept* your thanks.

Except: (preposition) excluding

I agree with all your assumptions *except* the last one.

Everyone went *except* him.

account for/to
Account for: (verb-preposition) to explain, to show what happened, to be responsible for

He must *account for* the increased petty cash spending.

Account to: (verb-preposition) to report to, answer to

He must *account to* us when he returns.

ad/add
Ad: (noun) short form of *advertisement*

Please bring me the *ad* from yesterday's paper.

Add: (verb) to calculate a total or sum; to attach

Please *add* the cost of shipping to the bill.

adapt/adopt
Adapt: (verb) to adjust or conform

I can *adapt* to any management style.

Adopt: (verb) to take, acquire, or accept

I will *adopt* your philosophy for handling complaints.

advice/advise
Advice: (noun) suggestions, recommendations, input

Do you have any *advice* for me on this project?

Advise: (verb) to suggest, to recommend, to have input

Can you *advise* me on this project?

affect/effect
Affect: (verb) to have an impact on

Will my work on this project *affect* my chances for promotion?

Effect: (noun) a result; (verb) to cause

Your speech had a tremendous *effect* on us. [Noun]

We cannot *effect* a change without your help. [Verb]

agree on/to/with
Agree on: (verb-preposition) to reach an understanding with someone about something that is named in the sentence

He and I *agree on* a new plan to solve the pollution problem.

Agree to: (verb-preposition) to give in or compromise, to undertake an action

We must *agree to* the terms of the contract.

Agree with: (verb-preposition) to reach an understanding with
someone

I *agree with* him.

ahold
This word does not exist in formal English.

Wrong: Please get *ahold* of Jones.

Rewrite: Please get *hold* of Jones.

                              or

                Please *contact* Jones.

aid/aide
Aid: (noun) assistance or help; (verb) to assist or to help

With your *aid*, I will finish this on time. [Noun]

Can I *aid* you in any way? [Verb]

Aide: (noun) one who helps, an assistant

Will you send your *aide* to help me tomorrow?

ain't/aren't
Ain't exists only in the most informal spoken English. *Aren't* is
an appropriate word at times:

Aren't we going to meet today?

We're going to meet today, *aren't* we?

At times, there is no contraction that can logically be used:

Wrong: I am going too, aren't I? [The subject *I* does not match the verb *are.*]

Rewrite: I am going too, am I not?

or

I am going too, right?

See sections 301-308, pages 33-40, for information on subject-verb agreement.

all of/off of
Usually you can delete the *of.*

Take *all* ~~*of*~~ the printouts.

All ~~*of*~~ the employees worked late yesterday.

Take those feet *off* ~~*of*~~ my desk, please.

I can't get that smudge *off* ~~*of*~~ our annual report.

See also section 323, page 64, for more information on unnecessary prepositions.

all ready/already
Use the adverb-adjective combination *all ready* when you mean *completely ready* or *all prepared.* Use the single word *already* when you mean *previously*:

He is *all ready* to go.

Has he *already* left?

all right/alright
Use *all right. Alright* is an error that probably arose from the common use of words such as *altogether* and *already.*

all together/altogether

Use the adverb-adjective combination *all together* when you mean *completely together.* Use the single word *altogether* when you mean *absolutely, entirely,* or *thoroughly:*

> We are *all together* in this proposal.

> I have *altogether* too much work to do.

all ways/always

Use the adjective-noun combination *all ways* when you mean *in every way.* Use the singular word *always* when you mean *all the time*:

> We are *in all ways* ready for this meeting.

> I *always* have too much work to do.

among/between

Use *among* to indicate a comparison or discussion that includes three or more people or things. Use *between* to indicate a comparison or discussion that includes two people or things:

> Let's keep our ideas *among* the three of us.

> Let's keep our ideas *between* the two of us.

Also use *between* with three or more people or things that are being considered in pairs and in a group:

> Place clips *between* the chapters of the report.

and etc./etc./and so on

Etc. means *and so on;* therefore, there is no need to write *and etc.*

> I'll need the usual office supplies: pens, paper, tape, stapler, *etc.*

Instead of the abbreviation *etc.,* use *and so on* in more formal writing. In the most formal writing, it is best not to use this construction at all but, rather, to introduce lists of examples with *such as.* Also, do not use *etc.* at the end of a series introduced by *such as.* The phrase *such as* implies that only representative examples will be given; therefore, it is unnecessary to add *etc.* or *and so on*, which suggest that further examples could be given.

See section 709, page 174, for common abbreviations.

and/or
The phrase *and / or* does not mean *either one or the other* but is appropriate only when three possibilities exist at the same time: (1) one of two things, (2) the other of two things, or (3) both things:

> Your reward will be a raise *and / or* a promotion. [The three options are a raise, a promotion, or both.]

anxious/eager
Anxious: (adjective) uneasy, concerned, worried

> She was *anxious* about her job review because she had not performed well the past six months.

Eager: (adjective) excited, enthusiastic

> She was *eager* for her job review because she had performed well the past six months.

any one/anyone
Use the adjective-pronoun combination *any one* when you mean *one of a number of people or things* and when a phrase beginning with *of* follows or is implied. Use the single word *anyone* in other cases:

> *Any one* of the four assistants might work well.

Anyone wanting vacation must let us know today.

Anyone can do that.

any time/anytime

Use the adjective-noun combination *any time* following prepositions such as *at*. Use the single word *anytime* when you mean *whenever*:

Feel free to call me at *any time*.

Anytime you are in town, stop at Gil's.

any way/anyway

Use the adjective-noun combination *any way* after prepositions such as *in*. Use the single word *anyway* when you mean *in any case* or *in any event:*

Feel free to call me if I can help in *any way*.

They really want you to stay. *Anyway*, you can't leave because you have a contract.

argue about/with

Argue about: (verb-preposition) to debate a topic or issue

We always *argue about* the new federal guidelines.

Argue with: (verb-preposition) to debate with another person

We always *argue with* the federal regulator.

as/like

Use *as* to connect two comparative clauses. Use *like* to connect two comparative words or phrases:

She comes from Los Angeles *as my previous boss did*. [Clause]

She is a Californian, *like me*. [Words]

She is a Californian, *like my previous boss*. [Phrases]

assure/ensure/insure

Use *assure* or *ensure* when referring to general guarantees, promises, and protections. *Assure* requires a direct object in the form of a person's name or a pronoun such as *him, her, you*. Use *insure* when referring to formal financial guarantees resulting in payment in case of death, illness, theft, accidents, and so on:

> I *assure* you that our products are fully warranted.

> You must *ensure* that your products are fully warranted.

> It costs only $2 per month to *insure* this jewelry.

bad/badly

Use the adjective *bad* when you wish to modify a noun or pronoun. Use the adverb *badly* when you wish to modify a verb or an adjective:

> He has a *bad* case of the jitters before every meeting. [Modifies the noun *case*.]

> I feel *bad*. [Modifies the pronoun *I*, not the verb *feel*. Saying "I feel badly" means that your sense of touch is poor.]

> I need a raise *badly*. [Modifies the verb *need*.]

> Those were *badly* needed sales. [Modifies the adjective *needed*.]

See section 318, page 55, for more information on adjectives and adverbs.

because/since

Generally, use *because* to express a cause-effect relationship, and use *since* to express a time relationship:

> I went to lunch early *because* I was hungry.

> Things haven't gone well *since* Bob left the department.

However, *since* can be used to mean *because* as long as the relationship in the sentence remains clear:

> *Since* I was hungry, I went to lunch early. [The cause-effect relationship is clearly expressed.]

beside/besides

Beside: (preposition) by, next to, near

> Put this in the file cabinet *beside* the desk.

Besides: (preposition) other than, together with, in addition to; (adverb) also, moreover

> *Besides* a new office, I'd like my own parking spot. [Preposition]

> I must be home by 5:30; *besides*, John does not mind if I leave early. [Adverb]

bi-/semi-

bi-: (prefix) two

> A *bi*weekly magazine comes every two weeks.

semi-: (prefix) half

> The *semi*annual report comes out every six months.

borrow/lend/loan

Borrow (verb): to take or accept something with the intention of returning it

> May I *borrow* a dollar?

Lend/loan: (verb) to give something, assuming that it will be returned

> Yes, I will *lend* you a dollar.

> Yes, I will *loan* you a dollar.

Loan: (noun) something given or taken with the understanding that it will be returned

> I asked him for a *loan*.

bring/take

Bring: (verb) to carry to or toward

> When you come, *bring* your son with you.

Take: (verb) to carry away from

> Please *take* these copies to Ralph.

> Please *take* these copies with you.

can/may

Use *can* to indicate ability; use *may* to indicate permission:

> I *can* key 90 words per minute.

> You *may* leave early on Friday.

capital/capitol

Capital: (adjective) excellent or primary, also the uppercase of alphabetic letters; (noun) the city in which the government is located

> Make that a *capital* letter. [Adjective]

We drove to the *capital*. [Noun]

Capitol: (noun) the actual building that houses governing bodies

> We toured the *capitol* yesterday, which was built in 1845.

choose/chose
Choose: (verb, present tense) to select or make a choice

> Which item do you *choose*?

Chose: (verb, past tense) selected, made a choice

> When she started here, she *chose* the corner office.

cite/site/sight
Cite: (verb) to acknowledge a reference or claim a source of information

> When you quote someone's words, you must *cite* the source of those words.

Site: (noun) a physical place, a piece of land

> You are standing on the *site* of the new MacGregor Building.

Sight: (noun) the ability to see; something that is seen

> The new MacGregor Building is a beautiful *sight*.

compare/contrast
Compare: (verb) to consider similarities and differences

> When we *compared* the two services, we found more similarities than differences.

Contrast: (verb) to consider differences

> When we *contrasted* the reports, we concluded that they had not been written by the same person.

complement/compliment
Complement: (verb) to complete or add to; (noun) that which completes or adds

> Your strengths *complement* mine; together, we are a good team. [Verb]

> A highly skilled assistant is the perfect *complement* to a good manager. [Noun]

Compliment: (verb) to say something nice, to make a flattering remark; (noun) a flattering remark

> I must *compliment* your handling of that situation. [Verb]

> You deserve a *compliment* for handling that situation so skillfully. [Noun]

continually/continuously
Continually: (adverb) repeatedly, happening frequently with brief interruption between occurrences

> The meeting was *continually* interrupted by phone calls.

Continuously: (adverb) nonstop, happening without interruption

> The president talked *continuously* during the meeting.

correspond to/with
Correspond to: (verb-preposition) to agree with something

Your final numbers do not *correspond to* mine.

Correspond with: (verb-preposition) to communicate with someone

Did you *correspond with* her before she moved here?

correspondence/correspondents
Correspondence: (noun) information that is exchanged, usually through writing

Please keep a file of all your *correspondence* with our clients.

Correspondents: (noun, plural) people who exchange information, usually through writing

He is one of my *correspondents.*

could of/should of/would of
The correct phrasing is *could have, should have,* and *would have.* The use of *of* is an error that probably comes from the pronunciation of the contractions for these phrases: *could've, should've,* and *would've:*

Wrong: I could of gone yesterday.

Rewrite: I *could have* gone yesterday.

or

I *could've* gone yesterday.

criteria/criterion
Criterion is singular; *criteria* is plural:

Our only *criterion* for choosing a new chairperson is knowledge of real estate policies and laws.

Do you meet all the *criteria* for filling this position?

data
Data (a noun) can be singular or plural, but is usually singular. If it refers to a single set of facts, data is singular. If it refers to more than one set, data is plural:

The *data* from the customer is not correct. [Singular]

The *data* from the three groups are not consistent. [Plural]

desert/dessert
Desert: (noun) an extremely dry geographical region; (verb) to escape, to abandon

To get to the seminar, we flew over the *desert*. [Noun]

Please do not *desert* us on the final day of the seminar. [Verb]

Dessert: (noun) the last course of a meal

The main course was excellent. May we order *dessert*? [Noun]

different from/different than
Use *from* when words and phrases represent contrasted elements; use *than* when the second contrasted element is a clause:

This office is *different from* mine.

This way of filing is *different from* our way.

His opinion is *different than* it was yesterday.

disinterested/uninterested
Disinterested: (adjective) impartial, objective

> Because the committee is divided, let's ask the
> opinion of a *disinterested* party.

Uninterested: (adjective) having no interest, not interested,
uncaring

> I'm completely *uninterested* in that project.

doesn't/don't Do not use *don't* (contraction of *do not*) when
doesn't (contraction of *does not*) should be used. Select the verb
do or *does* based on the corresponding subject:

Wrong: He *don't* work evenings.

Rewrite: He *doesn't* work evenings.

See sections 301–308, pages 33–40, for more information on
subject-verb agreement.

e.g./i.e.
e.g.: (prepositional phrase) for example

> Some of your suggestions (*e.g.*, that I plan step
> 2 only after step 1 is complete) were extremely
> helpful.

i.e.: (conjunction) that is

> The person you hire to replace me (*i.e.*, your new
> assistant) should prepare for at least two weeks
> of orientation to the job.

See section 709, page 174, for a list of common abbreviations.

every day/everyday
Use the adjective-noun combination *every day* when you mean

each day. Use the single word *everyday* when referring to that which is *routine, familiar,* or *commonplace*:

> For *every day* you stay, you build vacation time.

> You'll soon get used to the *everyday* procedures.

every one/everyone
Use the adjective-pronoun combination *every one* when you mean *each one of a number of people or things* and when a phrase beginning with *of* follows. Use the single word *everyone* in other cases:

> *Every one* of the suggestions will help increase productivity.

> For *every one* of those you buy, you receive a 5% rebate.

> *Everyone* must use his or her common sense.

farther/further
Farther: (adverb) more distant

> We will have to fly *farther* for next year's meeting.

Further: (adverb) in addition, moreover; to a greater degree or extent; (adjective) additional

> Let me take this example one step *further*. [Adverb]

> Should we allow *further* discussion? [Adjective]

fewer/less
Use *fewer* to modify nouns that can be counted; use *less* to modify nouns that cannot be counted:

> There were *fewer* people there than I expected.

There was *less* work to do on the project than I thought.

first/firstly
Use *first* (*second, third, last,* etc.), not *firstly. First* is already an adverb and, therefore, need not add -ly:

First, let me thank you for your time.

former/latter
Former: (adjective) first of two

Of his two ideas, I preferred the *former*. [The first.]

Latter: (adjective) second of two

Of his two ideas, I preferred the *latter*. [The second.]

good/well
Use the adjective *good* to modify a noun or pronoun; use the adverb *well* to modify a verb or adjective:

This is a *good* plan. [Modifies *plan*.]

This plan is *good*. [Modifies *plan*.]

She manages *well*. [Modifies *manages*.]

This is a *well* written letter. [Modifies *written*.]

See section 318, page 55, for more adjectives and adverbs that may be confused.

hear/here
Hear: (verb) to perceive sound through one's ears, to listen

Can you *hear* the speaker from the back of the room?

Here: (adverb) in or at this place

I cannot see the building from *here*.

if/whether
Use *if* to indicate a conditional relationship between two things. Use *whether* to indicate more than one alternative:

If he comes, I will leave. [Conditional relationship.]

She did not know *whether* to call or write a letter. [More than one alternative.]

imply/infer
Imply: (verb) to suggest something without stating it directly

Your letter *implies* that you are happy with your job.

Infer: (verb) to assume something not directly stated

I *infer* from your letter that you are happy with your job.

in/into, on/onto
Use *in* and *on* to indicate fixed positions or places. Use *into* and *onto* to indicate movement toward a position:

I'll wait *in* the parking ramp.

We're meeting *on* the second floor.

Go *into* the waiting room and have a seat.

She is moving *into* a management position next month.

He jumped *onto* my desk and yelled, "It's Friday!"

Note: Do not use the single words *into* and *onto* when the two-word phrases *in to* and *on to* are needed:

> Turn your reports *in to* Walter. [*In* is an adverb modifying *turn,* and *to* is the preposition.]

> The crowd left, but he went *on to* finish his speech. [*On* is an adverb modifying *went,* and *to* is part of the phrase *to finish.*]

> Don't go *on to* the next topic yet. [*On* is an adverb modifying *go,* and *to* is the preposition.]

See section 321, page 62, for more information on distinguishing prepositions and adverbs.

irregardless/regardless

Use *regardless. Irregardless* is not a word; *ir-* and *-less* both indicate *not* or *without,* so *irregardless* is, in a sense, a double negative:

> *Regardless* of your complaint, I cannot refund your money without your receipt.

is when/is where

Do not use the phrases *is when* or *is where* to introduce definitions of nouns (or verbal phrases used as nouns). Instead, use nouns or noun phrases to define nouns:

Wrong: Data entry *is when* you key information into the database.

A conference call *is where* more than two parties speak from various locations.

Rewrite: Data entry is the keying of information into the database.

A conference call is a telephone call during which more than two parties speak from various locations.

it's/its
Use *it's* when you mean *it is* or *it has*. Use *its* when you want to show possession:

> *It's* not fair that she earns more than I earn.

> *It's* been a long time since we met.

> The committee submitted *its* report.

last/latest/past
Last: (adjective) final, concluding

> This is the *last* time I will answer that question.

Latest: (adjective) most recent, newest, current

> Our *latest* sales figures suggest we are going strong.

Past: (adjective) former, previous, prior

> Our *past* president did not have the skills of our current president.

lay/lie
Lay: (verb, always takes object) to place something down

>   obj
> Please *lay* the file on my desk.

> He *is laying* the file on my desk.

past tense: laid

> He *laid* the file on my desk yesterday.

perfect tense: laid (with helping verb)

> He *has laid* the file on my desk before.

Lie: (verb, never takes object) to recline; to give false information

Please *lie* on the table until the doctor comes.

I *am lying* on the table.

past tense: lay

Yesterday I *lay* on the table for two hours.

perfect tense: lain (with helping verb)

In the last two weeks, I *have lain* on this table for more than two hours.

Tenses of the verb *lie* meaning *to give false information* are *lie/lying* (present), *lied* (past), and *lied* (perfect). *See section 310, page 42, for information on forms of difficult verbs.*

lead/led
Lead: (noun) type of metal

Let's replace those old *lead* pipes next year.

Lead: (verb) to take charge, to be in a position of authority

Because of your skills, we would like you to *lead* the group discussion.

Led: (verb) took charge, was in position of authority

You *led* yesterday's discussion exceptionally well.

literally

This word means the same as *actually, precisely*, or *truly*. Do not use it incorrectly to introduce an exaggeration:

> I was *literally* offered the world to work here!
> [Delete *literally*.]

> She will *literally* faint when she sees that!
> [Delete *literally*.]

loose/lose

Loose: (adjective) not fully or properly connected or attached

> No wonder the printer won't work. The cable is *loose*.

Lose: (verb) to mislay, misplace, confuse, or forget; to be defeated

> Don't *lose* those screws when you take the cover off.

> We cannot *lose* that account!

> If I don't sell more, I'll *lose* the contract.

media/medium

Medium is singular; *media* is plural:

> Is the lecture the best *medium* through which to train our staff?

> Are lecture and small-group discussion the best *media* through which to train our staff?

Miss/Mrs./Ms.

Miss refers to an unmarried female, and *Mrs.* refers to a married female. There are no similar ways to distinguish a man's marital status, and many people now use *Ms.* as the female equivalent of *Mr.* Use *Ms.* (pronounced "Miz") unless you are certain a person prefers *Miss* or *Mrs.*

moot/mute

Moot: (adjective) debatable; insignificant

> That is a *moot* point, with which I disagree.

> Since the policy has already been written and approved, your argument is *moot.*

Mute: (adjective) unable to speak or be heard

> Even though the actor was *mute*, he was able to communicate with the audience.

moral/morale

Moral: (adjective) spiritually or ethically correct

> Our security guards must have the highest *moral* character.

Morale: (noun) general feeling or attitude

> Our staff's *morale* has improved considerably since we eliminated daily reporting requirements.

more important/more importantly

Use *more important,* which is a short form for *What is more important*:

> I found the missing information. *More important*, the information supports your position on next year's budget.

no body/nobody

Use the adjective-noun combination *no body* when you mean *no group within a larger group.* Use the single word *nobody* when referring to individuals:

No body of the government can act alone to make a law.

Nobody can get into the building on weekends.

off of
See *all of*.

on/onto
See *in / into*.

oral/verbal
Oral: (adjective) by mouth, spoken

> We have an *oral* contract.

Verbal: (adjective) relating to words, either spoken or written

> Her *verbal* skills are excellent.

passed/past
Passed: (verb) sent, threw, handed; went beyond or through

> She *passed* a note to her assistant during the meeting.

> He *passed* the training course with no problem.

Past: (adjective) lapsed, expired; (noun) period of time before the present; (adverb) beyond

> The high-volume buying period is *past*. [Adjective]

> In the *past*, we have had only two or three sales reps. [Noun]

> Your payment is *past* due. [Adverb]

See also *last / latest / past*.

peace/piece
Peace: (noun) condition of harmony; lacking conflict

> Once he retires, we should have *peace* again in
> our department.

Piece: (noun) portion or fragment; (verb) to put something
together into a larger whole

> I need only one more *piece* of paper. [Noun]

> You can probably *piece* together your report
> from these other reports. [Verb]

people/persons
Use *people* as the plural form of *person*.

> Twenty *people* attended the meeting.

percent/percentage
Use *percent* to express a specific figure. Use *percentage* to
express the general concept:

> They gave us *8 percent*.

> I need *4.5 percent* just to keep up with the cost
> of living.

> What *percentage* will we need to compete?

> If a large *percentage* of people vote, I will win.

personal/personnel
Personal: (adjective) relating to or belonging to an individual
person, private

> Our Employee Assistance Program helps those
> whose *personal* problems are affecting their
> work.

Personnel: (noun) a group of employees; (adjective) relating to a group of employees

> Our *personnel* have all received academic degrees. [Noun]

> Our *personnel* department keeps detailed records on sick leave and vacation. [Adjective]

plus
Do not use *plus* as a conjunction replacing *and*:

Wrong: He wanted a new word processor *plus* a new printer.

> She went to see the Capitol, *plus* they both toured the White House.

Rewrite: He wanted a new word processor *and* a new printer.

> She went to see the Capitol, *and* they both toured the White House.

precede/proceed
Precede: (verb) to come before or ahead of

> The keynote address will *precede* the workshops.

Proceed: (verb) to move forward or ahead

> Once you have turned left onto Federal Avenue, *proceed* north until you see the Brewer Building.

principal/principle
Principal: (adjective) main or most important; (noun) a sum of money; a school administrator

> My *principal* concern is that I won't have enough time. [Adjective]

The mutual fund offered a high interest rate on our *principal*. [Noun]

We talked to the *principal* about our school starting a business club. [Noun]

Principle: (noun) concept, idea, rule, belief

This is a difficult *principle* to understand.

Open communication is one of the *principles* of good management.

raise/rise

Raise: (verb, always takes an object) to lift or increase *something* to a higher level

obj
Please consider *raising* my *salary* in January.

past tense: raised

Ms. Wilt *raised* my salary last month.

perfect tense: raised (with helping verb)

Ms. Wilt *has raised* my salary twice before.

Rise: (verb, never takes an object) to move upward or increase

If my salary continues to *rise*, I'll be well paid soon.

past tense: rose

When my salary *rose* last month, I paid off that loan.

perfect tense: risen (with helping verb)

My salary *has risen* only twice in three years.

See section 310, page 42, for information on difficult verb forms.

real/really

Do not use the adjective *real* when you should use the adverb *really* to modify an adjective:

Wrong: This is a *real* big problem.

Rewrite: This is a *really* big problem.

See section 318, page 55, for more adjectives and adverbs that may be confused.

reason/reason is because/reason why

Reason is because and *reason why* are redundant phrases. Avoid using them:

Original: The *reason* I left *is because* I wanted to work alone.

                          or

              The *reason why* I left is that I wanted to work alone.

Rewrite: The *reason* I left *is* that I wanted to work alone.

                          or

              I left *because* I wanted to work alone.

set/sit

Set: (verb, always takes an object) to place *something* down

                          obj
              Please *set* the file *cabinet* in the corner.

past tense: set

She *set* the file cabinet in the corner yesterday.

perfect tense: set (with helping verb)

She *has set* the file cabinet in the corner twice before.

Sit: (verb, never takes an object) to be seated or to remain in place

Please *sit* in the waiting room until I call.

past tense: sat

I *sat* in the waiting room yesterday.

perfect tense: sat (with helping verb)

I have *sat* in the waiting room many times before.

See section 310, page 42, for information on difficult verb forms.

shall/will
Use *will*. *Shall* is now used so seldom that it may be considered obsolete.

should of
See *could of.*

simple/simplistic
Simple: (adjective) easy

This task was *simple*.

Simplistic: (adjective) too simple, overly simplified

Your thinking on this is *simplistic*.

some day/someday

Use the adjective-noun combination *some day* when it follows a preposition. Use the single word *someday* to refer to *an unspecified future day:*

> *Please set up a meeting for some day* next week.

> *but*

> *Someday* I will finish this project.

> We will get a new supervisor *someday.*

some time/sometime/sometimes

Use the adjective-noun combination *some time* when the word *time* can be used alone. Use the single word *sometime* to mean *an unspecified future time.* Use the single word *sometimes* to mean *at times* or *once in a while*:

> Please give me *some time* to respond.

> I can call *sometime* tomorrow, if necessary.

> *Sometimes* I like to work alone.

stationary/stationery

Stationary: (adjective) without movement

> He exercises on a *stationary* bike.

Stationery: (noun) paper on which letters are sent, often with matching envelopes

> Please order more company *stationery.*

supposed to/used to

In sentences requiring a past tense verb, do not use the present tense:

> *Wrong:*   We were *suppose* to check in early.

After a while, we were *use* to it.

Rewrite: We were *supposed to* check in early.

After a while, we were *used to* it.

than/then
Than: (conjunction) in comparison with, when compared with

Her office is much larger *than* mine.

Then: (adverb) at that time, after that, next

Find Mr. Peters first and *then* call me.

that/which/who/whose
Use *that* with essential modifying clauses and *which* with nonessential modifying clauses. Use *who* with essential or nonessential modifying clauses that refer to people. Use *whose* with essential or nonessential modifying clauses that show possession, whether referring to a person or an object:

He wanted the file *that* was on the desk. [Essential: The *that* clause tells which file he wants, distinguishing it from other files.]

He wanted the file, *which* was on the desk. [Nonessential: The *which* clause implies that there is only one file. Its location is additional, but not necessary, information.]

We must identify the assistant *who* can write the best copy. [Essential]

She asked for Hal, *who* can write the best copy. [Nonessential]

We must identify the assistant *whose* writing skills are the best. [Essential]

Let's ask Sally, whose skills we know we can trust. [Nonessential]

See also section 414, page 77, for more information on essential and nonessential modifiers.

their/there/they're
Their: (pronoun) belonging to them

> *Their* office complex is just what we need.

There: (adverb) in or at that place

> The one we need is over *there*.

> *There* are two more files in the drawer.

They're: (contraction) they are

> *They're* the ones who will be moving out.

theirselves/themselves
The correct choice is *themselves*:

Wrong: They probably find *theirselves* very busy at times.

Rewrite: They probably find *themselves* very busy at times.

till/until/'til/'till
Till and *until* are interchangeable; however, *until* is more broadly accepted and should be used in formal writing. *'Til* is a contraction for *until* and should be used only informally. *'Till* is an error that probably reflects a combination of the other forms.

to/too/two
To: (preposition) in the direction of, toward

> Take me *to the supply closet.*

Too: (adverb) extremely, very; also

This report is *too* long.

This report must be sent *too*.

Two: (adjective) 2

I'll take *two* copies, please.

See section 312, page 46, for information on using *to* with verbs.

try and
Use *try to* or simply *try*, not *try and*:

Wrong: *Try and* find the Smithers file.

Rewrite: *Try to* find the Smithers file.

or

Try finding the Smithers file.

unique
Reserve this to mean one of a kind, not simply different or unusual.

All three of us have *unique* working styles. [The writer probably means unusual or different, obviously not one of a kind.]

weather/whether
Weather: (noun) the climate, usually outdoors

What will the *weather* be like in Florida?

Whether: (conjunction) See *if/whether*.

I don't know *whether* or not I should go.

who/whom/whoever/whomever
Use *who* and *whoever* in the nominative case, usually as the

subject of a clause. Use *whom* and *whomever* in the objective case, usually as the object of a clause or of a prepositional phrase:

> *Who* is coming?

> I am the one *who* found the money.

> *Whoever* works overtime must talk with our accountant.

> Give it to *whoever* asks first. [Here the clause beginning with *whoever* is the object of the preposition *to*. Because *whoever* is the subject of the clause, it is in the nominative case.]

> *Whom* did you say was coming?

> To *whom* were you speaking?

> You did that to *whom*?

> Tell *whomever* you wish.

See section 314, page 51, for descriptions of pronoun cases.

who's/whose
Use *who's* when you mean *who is* or *who has*. Use *whose* when you want to show possession:

> *Who's* going to join our conference call?

> *Who's* been misfiling this information?

> *Whose* job is that?

See also *that / which / who / whose*.

-wise
This suffix is added to many words to form an adverb; however, avoid this suffix when you write because there is almost always a better way to say what you mean:

Original: We are doing fine moneywise.

Rewrite: We are doing fine financially.

or

We have enough money.

with/within
Use *with* to indicate that someone or something is in the company or presence of another. Use *within* to indicate that one thing is inside of another or is encompassed by another:

  I'll go *with* you tomorrow.

  The Daltry file is on my desk *with* the Ames file.

  The solution to your problem lies *within* this proposal.

  Most people receive promotions *within* their own companies.

would of
See *could of.*

you're/your
Use *you're* when you mean *you are.* Use *your* when you want to show possession:

  You're not going with us tomorrow.

  Your work on this report must be finished by Monday.

Below is an alphabetical list of often used office technology
words and phrases. Words that are italicized in the definitions
also appear in the alphabetized list. For words not listed here,
check a current dictionary or the documentation for your
equipment. For a list of the most frequently used DOS
commands, see appendix A.

access	to call up information that is stored on a *disk*
application software	program containing sets of instructions that enable the computer to perform a specific function such as *word processing*, *graphics* design, *spreadsheet* creation, or communicating with other computers
bar code reader	scanning device that analyzes the light and dark bars that appear on products and translates them into electrical signals for the computer; also used in filing systems to track paper and other media
batch	group of data that can be processed using a single operation
bit	smallest unit of information that can be recognized by a computer; combined to form *characters*
boilerplate	standard form or a standard part of a document stored on *disk* to be used repeatedly with, perhaps, slight modification each time
boot	to activate a computer and prepare it to run a *program*
buffer	see *clipboard*

byte	eight *bits*, the number of *bits* required to form a *character*
CD-ROM	Compact Disk-Read Only Memory; a storage medium, read by a *laser disk* drive, containing large *databases* of information including text, voice, and video
cell	area of a *spreadsheet* where a column and row meet
character	single letter, number, space, or other symbol that is represented in a computer
chip	circuit that is placed in a computer, allowing the computer to process information
clipboard	block of *memory* that holds data temporarily
communications program	electronic set of instructions for sending and receiving information through a *modem*
computer-aided design (CAD)	the application of computer technology to the design process enabling the user to create three-dimensional drawings to scale
configuration	(1) the combination of *hardware* that makes up a computer station, usually consisting of at least a *CPU*, a *monitor*, and a keyboard; (2) how the hardware is set up (its capacity, its operating system, etc.)
CPU	Central Processing Unit; the box that houses the *chips*

CRT	Cathode-Ray Tube; the computer's *monitor*
cursor	flashing, floating character on the computer screen that indicates where keyed data will be placed on the monitor
database	collection of interrelated information that may be organized and sorted electronically
data communications	information transmitted through wires, usually phone wires
data processing	computerized collecting, storing, manipulating, and sending of data
desktop publishing (DTP)	production of designed and formatted documents, including books and magazines, using a personal computer; includes the ability to incorporate graphics into the text
directory	in a computer's electronic filing system, a specially designated area for storing files
disk(ette)	storage medium for information; may be internal (*hard disk*) or external (*floppy disk* or *laser disk*)
disk drive	a piece of *hardware* (inside or outside of *CPU*) that allows the computer to *read* and write to *disk*
disk operating system	see *DOS*

documentation	written or printable information and instructions that accompany computer *hardware* and *software*
DOS	Disk Operating System; *software* that contains the *programs* and instructions that manage and supervise a computer system
dot matrix	see *printer*
EGA monitor	Enhanced Graphic Adapter; a monitor that can display up to 64 text colors and has better resolution than the original color monitors
e-mail	electronic mail; the ability to send written messages from one *terminal* to another within the same computer *network*
electronic mail	see *e-mail*
facsimile	see *fax*
fax	a machine that converts written messages or graphics into signals that can be sent over telephone lines
fiber optic cable	clear, flexible tubing within which light impulses transmit data quickly with few errors
field	a category of information in a *database*
floppy disk	an external magnetic *disk(ette)*
footer	a small amount of text (usually one to three lines) automatically printed at the bottom of selected pages of a document

font	a specific type size and style of a character
full-page display	the ability of a computer *monitor* to display the equivalent of a full sheet of standard paper
function key	a single key or two-key combination on a computer keyboard that is programmed to a specific operation, such as saving or printing
Gb	Gigabyte, 1 billion *characters*; used to specify the storage capacity of a computer
global	describes an operation that affects an entire file or document; for example, a global search is an electronic search of an entire file or document
grammar checker	see *style checker*
graphic user interface	an *icon*-based *software program* that allows users to run *software programs* simultaneously and move or copy information between *programs* without quitting one *program* and starting another
graphics	information communicated primarily through nonalphabetical symbols, such as tables, charts, graphs, and design elements
hard copy	a printed version of a document created with a computer program
hard disk	see *disk(ette)*

hardware   the equipment, other than *software*, required to process data on a computer: *CPU*, *monitor*, *printer*, and so on

header   a small amount of text (usually one to three lines) automatically printed at the top of selected pages of a document

host computer   a computer dedicated to controlling a *network* and providing most of the data storage; also, *server*

icon   a small graphic representing a *software* application, computer operation, function, or file found primarily in *graphic user interface* software

ink jet printer   see *printer*

input   information that is keyed or otherwise fed into a computer

integrated software   *program* that includes more than one *software* application and allows the easy transfer of data from one application to another

interface   the connection made between separate pieces of *hardware* or between *hardware* and *software*

justification   the process of spacing between letters or words to create an even right margin (right justification), an even left margin (left justification), even left and right margins (full justification); or centered text (center justification)

K (or Kb)	abbreviation for Kilobyte, 1,000 *characters*; used to specify the storage capacity of a computer
LAN	Local Area Network; a computer network made up of *workstations* (or *terminals*) in a geographically close area (usually the same building) that are wired together to allow the exchange of data
laptop	a compact, portable *microcomputer*
laser disk	an information-storage medium requiring a disk drive that reads and writes using light; often called *optical disk*
laser printer	see *printer*
LCD	Liquid Crystal Display; a type of display used in many computer instruments, digital watches, and calculators to show numerical and alphabetical characters; an example is a device that projects images from a computer monitor to a wall or screen for viewing by larger audiences
letter-quality printer	*printer* that produces high-quality output suitable for formal distribution
light pen	a pen-shaped *input* device that activates *software* functions by simply touching the *monitor*
local area network	see *LAN*
macro	a single computer instruction created by a user to replace a sequence of operations

mainframe	the most powerful class of computers; usually used by large organizations for storing and manipulating *databases*; can serve as a *host computer* for a *local area network*
main memory	see *RAM*
Mb	Megabyte, 1 million *characters*; used to specify the storage capacity of a computer
memory	the capacity of a computer to store information for future use
menu	a software feature that displays a list of processing options
merge	to combine one document (or part of one document) with another
micro-computer	personal computer; a computer that uses a microprocessor as its central control; distinguished from *minicomputers* and *mainframe* computers
mini-computer	medium-sized computer (more powerful than a *microcomputer* but less powerful than a *mainframe*); its role in a business is similar to that of a *mainframe*
modem	a piece of *hardware* that allows a computer to interface with another computer by way of telephone lines
monitor	computer screen
mother board	the main circuit board inside the central processing unit (*CPU*) of the computer

mouse	a hand-sized desktop device by which a computer operator can move the *cursor* and perform command operations without using the keyboard
NLQ	Near Letter Quality; describes high-quality *dot matrix* printing (see *printer*)
network	a computer setup in which *terminals* or *workstations* are wired together to allow the exchange of data (see *LAN* and *WAN*)
OCR	Optical Character Recognition; the means by which a *scanner* interprets printed characters and converts them electronically to a form that can be stored directly into a computer's memory
offline	the operating state of a printer that is not ready to receive commands or print
online	the operating state of a printer that is ready to receive commands and print
operating system	the set of commands that allows the computer to function, to run *software*, and to process information
optical disk	see *laser disk*
output	what the computer produces after processing the *input*
parallel transmission	a way computers and *peripherals* exchange information; allows an entire *character* or *byte* to be sent simultaneously (instead of one *bit* at a time, as in *serial transmission*)

parent directory   a *directory* made up of subdirectories

peripherals   *hardware* that is added to the *CPU* for *input* and *output,* such as a keyboard, *monitor, printer*, and *mouse*

personal information system   *software* that helps computer users manage time and maintain schedules

pica   a unit of measure for printed *characters*; there are 6 picas to the inch

point   a unit of a *pica*; there are 12 points in 1 *pica*

printer   a piece of *hardware* that provides a *hard copy* of information or text processed by a computer

                  dot matrix   impact printer that produces readable text and *graphics* by forming each *character* with a series of ink dots

                  ink jet   *letter-quality* or near letter-quality printer that produces *characters* by spraying the paper with tiny dots of ink

                  laser   printer that produces high-quality text and graphics by focusing a laser beam on the surface of a light-sensitive drum and recording the image in the form of tiny dots

printer driver   file that works with the *software* application and the computer *hardware* to generate printed reports

program	a set of instructions that allows a computer to perform its operations
programming	writing the commands that allow a computer to perform its operations
prompt	a *character* on the screen (often a > or a *cursor*) that lets a computer operator know the computer is ready for a command or for data *input*
proportional spacing	text spacing in which the amount of space taken by a letter is based on the size of the *character*
protocols	the set of rules that regulate the way data is transmitted between *workstations* or *terminals* in a network
query	request for selected information in a *database* program
RAM	Random Access Memory; short-term active memory in which programs and data reside when they are being used; information left in RAM is lost when the computer is turned off
random access memory	see *RAM*
read	the term given to the operation in which the computer signals the disk drives to scan a *disk* to find data
relational database	a database structure that links information through a common *field*
remote terminal	in a network controlled by a host computer (a *minicomputer* or a *mainframe* computer),

a *terminal* located at a site distant from the host computer

ROM Read Only Memory; memory in which a computer's permanent programs (programs that control the basic computer functions) are stored; programs stored in ROM cannot be altered

root directory the main *directory* on a *disk*

scanner see *OCR*; a device that scans printed text or *graphics* and converts the images to a form that can be directly *input* into a computer's memory

scroll to move the image that appears on the computer screen up, down, right, or left

search and replace a word processing operation by which the computer locates every instance of selected data and replaces it with another piece of data

serial transmission a way computers and *peripherals* exchange information back and forth; information is sent one *bit* at a time (instead of an entire *character* or *byte* at once, as in *parallel transmission*)

server see *host computer*

soft copy information or data that is stored on a computer *disk* or displayed on the monitor

software electronic instructions (programs, such as *word processing*, *spreadsheet*, *database*, and *desktop publishing* applications) and data used in computer operations; distinct

	from *hardware*, such as the *CPU, monitor,* keyboard, and *printer*
source disk	a *disk* that contains the data being copied
spell checker	a component of a *word processing* program that analyzes text and highlights words or groups of *characters* that do not appear in its programmed word list (dictionary)
split screen	a feature that can divide the *monitor* display so the computer operator can view two separate documents or two separate sections of a single document
spreadsheet	*application software* that performs mathematical calculations and is often used for storing and manipulating numerical data and for presenting data in tabular form
stand-alone system	a system of *hardware* and *software* that can operate fully without the assistance of another *terminal* or computer
storage	the ability of a computer to save and store data
style checker	a *software* program usually used with a *word processing* program for analyzing written text to highlight possible errors and suggest possible revisions
super computer	most powerful of all computers; used for such things as aviation simulations, medical research, and weather forecasting
target disk	*disk* that receives copied data

telecommunica-tions	electronic communication of information over a distance, commonly by way of telephone lines, satellite transmission, or microwave transmission
template	cardboard or plastic plate that fits over the keyboard and contains a command summary; sometimes also used to mean *boilerplate*
Tb	Terabyte, 1 trillion *characters*; used to indicate the storage capacity of a computer
terminal	a single computer *workstation*, often *networked* to a *minicomputer* or *mainframe*
VGA monitor	Video Graphic Adapter; *monitor* that can display information in *graphic* form
video disk	large *laser disk* that combines video images with sound; connects to computer for information retrieval
WAN	Wide Area Network; a network in which computers from different locations are connected through microwave, satellite, or telephone transmission
warm boot	*booting software* when the *hardware* is already turned on
word processing	a computer software application that allows the operator to create correspondence and other text documents that can be easily edited

workstation	formerly used to refer to computer terminals connected in a network and controlled by a *minicomputer* or *mainframe*, now often used for any computer *terminal* in a business environment
WORM	Write Once-Read Many; *laser disk* system that allows computers to write to the disk once but never change the information
WMRM	Write Many-Read Many; *laser disk* system that allows computers to read and write to the disk repeatedly, as with magnetic media (*floppy disk* and *hard disk*)
wraparound	the ability of most *word processing* programs to begin a new line automatically when a line has reached the right margin
WYSIWYG	What You See Is What You Get; means that information will appear on paper just as it looks on the monitor

NOTES

BUSINESS DOCUMENTS
- Business Letters
- Interoffice Memorandums
- Meeting Agendas and Minutes
- Business Reports

NOTES

BUSINESS DOCUMENTS

Part 10 provides guidelines for formatting letters, memos, reports, agendas, meeting minutes, outlines, and tables. These guidelines represent widely accepted standards rather than inflexible rules, and circumstances may dictate that other standards be observed. However, two primary goals to consider when formatting business documents are (1) readability—achieving an overall balanced appearance—and (2) completeness—including all required information. All formatting decisions should consider these two goals.

BUSINESS LETTERS

Letter Styles `1001`

Business letters are formatted in one of three styles: block, modified block, or simplified:

a. Block Style. The block style is recommended for its efficiency and streamlined appearance. The block-style letter begins each letter part and paragraph at the left margin (see figure 10.1).

b. Modified Block Style. The indented date, complimentary close, and signature block of this style allows some formatting flexibility, especially to balance letterhead that may be flush with the left margin (see figure 10.2).

c. Simplified Style. By using a subject line to replace the salutation, this letter style provides a comfortable option when writing to groups or to people whose names you do not know. Note that this style does not use a complimentary close (see figure 10.3).

See section 1002, page 259, for information on letter formatting.

Return address	**_Proofreading Plus_**
Vertically centered on page	1234 West Mountain Drive • Los Angeles, CA 67676-1111 • (333) 555-8898 Fax (333) 555-7999
Date line	November 15, 19XX **5 returns**
Inside address	Ms. Rochelle Andoian, President Advanced Design Consultants 8800 Susquehanna Lane Bryn Mawr, PA 15221 **2 returns**
Colon after salutation	Dear Ms. Andoian: **2 returns**
1-inch margins	You are right! The correspondence your firm prepares sends its own message. Thus, you will want to send a clear message of efficiency as illustrated by this block-style letter. **Double space**
Left justification (ragged right)	All lines begin at the left margin. The date begins approximately 12 lines from the top of the page. The inside address begins four lines below the date. Margins of 1" are used. The letter is single-spaced with double spacing before and after the salutation, between paragraphs, and before the complimentary close. The writer's name appears on the fourth line below the closing. Reference initials and a filename are placed two lines below the sender's name. **Double Space** The block letter has grown considerably in popularity. This is no doubt due to its inherent efficiency.
Comma after closing	Sincerely, **4 returns**
Sender's name and title	Teresa Gomez, Account Executive Accounting Department **2 returns**
Reference initials/filename	wg/block.ltr

Fig. 10.1. Recommended letter style: block style.

**SOUTHERN
COMMUNICATION
ASSOCIATION**

2583 Magnolia • Atlanta, GA 09876-1255 • (255) 555-6767 Fax (255) 555-6788

**Date line begins at
center**

November 15, 19XX **2 returns**

When replying, refer to: File 592 **3 returns**

Refer to line

Administrative Secretaries Association
P.O. Box 5500
Austin, TX 78710 **2 returns**

**Left justification
(ragged right)**

Dear Colleagues: **2 returns**

Your recent inquiry regarding letter styles endorsed by the
Southern Communication Association was very timely. Our
group is in the process of assembling a business letter
style guide for office support persons. This letter is the
first sample for the guide.

This letter illustrates the modified block style. Default
side margins of 1" are used. The date begins approximately
12 lines from the top of the page at center. The inside
address begins four lines below the date line. A double
line space precedes and follows the salutation. The
message of the letter is single-spaced with double spacing
between paragraphs.

The complimentary close begins a double space below the
body at center. The writer's name and title appear four
lines below, aligned with the closing. The reference
notation is positioned two lines below the signature line
at the left margin. **2 returns**

Sincerely yours, **4 returns**

**Closing and keyed
signature begin at
center**

Theodore A. Gullman
Corresponding Secretary **2 returns**

trw/modblock.let

**Fig. 10.2. Modified block style, showing 1-inch margins,
left justification, and *Refer to* line.**

George Burkett Associates, Inc.

One Crystal Palace
99 Nicollet Mall
Minneapolis, MN 09888-3333
(111) 555-3970 Fax (111) 555-3622

November 15, 19XX

Alternative Energies Corporation
1250 Gulfside Drive
Biloxi, MS 39535   3 returns

Subject line   SIMPLIFIED LETTER STYLE   3 returns

Because you are considered a trend setter in the energy
conservation field, we recommend that your corporation use
this simplified letter style when appropriate.

Note the special features of this style. The salutation is
replaced by an all-caps subject line. (The word "Subject"
is not used.) The closing block omits the complimentary
close; the writer's name and title appear in all caps.

Default margins of 1" are used. Paragraphs are blocked. A
triple space is used above and below the subject line. The
signature line appears at the left margin four lines below
the body of the letter.

We think your staff will like the clean, contemporary look
of this style. 4 returns

No closing

Sender's name   PATRICIA E. HOEKSTRA, ACCOUNT EXECUTIVE
and title
capitalized   hg/simplfd.let

Fig. 10.3. Simplified letter style.

Achieving a balanced overall appearance to enhance readability is the primary goal of letter formatting. *See section 1003, page 264, for a list of specific letter parts and corresponding sections.*

a. Spacing. Generally, single-space business letters, but double-space between paragraphs. See figures 10.1, 10.2, and 10.3 for spacing between letter parts.

b. Margins. For a balanced appearance, letters should have equal margins on the left and right; the top and bottom margins should be approximately equal, with the bottom margin two or three spaces greater than the top. See figure 10.2 for an example of even margins.

Usually, you cannot accurately judge how much space the body of a letter will occupy until you have keyed it. Therefore, key your letter first, assuming 1" left and right margins; then adjust the vertical placement (top and bottom margins) as needed. If adjusting vertical placement is not enough—that is, if top and bottom margins appear too large—adjust the left and right margins as necessary between .75" and 1.5" (*see section 1002d, page 260*).

Tech Tip

When you finish keying a letter, use the feature of your software that displays the layout of the letter. If the text appears unusually high or low on the page, make adjustments before printing (*see 1002d, page 260*). Also, you can use a Center Page feature to create a visually centered letter.

---

c. Justification. A ragged right edge aids readability because no unnecessary spacing appears within lines of text. Use left justification (ragged right edge) for business letters (see figure 10.2).

d. Adjusting Format for Long or Short Letters. To achieve a balanced appearance, exceptionally long or short letters may require margin or spacing adjustments, for example:

- Place the date higher or lower on the page.
- Delete space between the date and the inside address.
- Adjust side margins from .75" minimum to 1.5 " maximum.
- Delete space between the complimentary close and the writer's signature line, leaving enough space for the signature.
- Allow long letters to go beyond a single page.

See figure 10.4 for an example of a short letter formatted for balance.

When a letter goes beyond a single page, use a header on all pages after the first to avoid confusion if the pages become separated (see figure 10.5). In addition, make sure isolated words or lines of text (often called *widows* and *orphans*) do not begin or end a page.

See sections 1004–1019, pages 264–279, for other formatting issues related to specific letter parts. See sections 1024, page 281, and 1033, page 303, for information on formatting memos and reports. See sections 205–206, pages 28–29, for information on proofreading a document's appearance and on proofreaders' marks.

If your word processing package has a Widow/Orphan Protect feature, you can use it to ensure that no single words or lines appear at the top or bottom of a page.

e. Word Division.

See sections 822–831, pages 195–198, for information on dividing words at the ends of lines in business documents.

November 15, 19XX   **5 returns**

Pets Unlimited
612 Brock Creek Road
Butte, MT 59701   **3 returns**

CATALOG REQUEST   **3 returns**

Would you please send me a copy of your latest
catalog of pet supplies.

I am particularly interested in two items: (1) dog
collars personalized with the pet's name and
telephone number embossed and (2) holiday cards
featuring an English springer spaniel.   **4 returns**

JANE BRYANT
Return address   3434 Parkway Lane
Asheville, NC 29825
(714) 555-8765

**Fig. 10.4. Short letter with format adjustments for
balanced appearance, showing return address position
without letterhead.**

Creative Fund-Raising Inc.

5656 Maryland Parkway   (913) 555-8989
Topeka, KS 66610   Fax (913) 555-8992

February 14, 19XX

Ms. Alicia Webber, President   Mr. Albert Donworth, Manager
Midwest Bottlers Corporation   Midwest Bottlers Corporation
156 Central Boulevard   P.O. Box 770
Kansas City, KS 87230   Blair, NB 63890

Dear Ms. Webber and Mr. Donworth:

Thank you for the opportunity to work with your firm to achieve our recycling and fund-raising goals. We are proud to be associated with a forward-thinking company such as yours and look forward to working with you throughout the year.

Our first month's pickup at your headquarters yielded some interesting results. As you requested, we will share them with you here. As you can see from the table below, we collected a total of 756 pounds of recyclables from your office. Since no recycling collection is completely successful, we estimate that your total consumption of the four recyclables below is approximately 835 pounds per month. Of the total we were able to collect, office paper made up more than one-third while hard plastic made up less than one-eighth of the total. Since office paper is relatively easy to recycle and hard plastic is relatively difficult to recycle, this contrast is positive.

RECYCLABLE	POUNDS	% OF TOTAL
Office Paper	270	35.7
Hard Plastic	93	12.3
Aluminum	181	24.0
Glass	212	28.0
	756	100

Based on these results, we recommend that you and your employees take the following steps to decrease both your recyclable and nonrecyclable waste:

In the left margin:

Two people at different addresses

Table cited in text for clarity

Centered table

Page break without leaving single line of text

Fig. 10.5. Multiple-page letter with more than one mailing address, a table, and numbered paragraphs.

Ms. Alicia Webber
Mr. Albert Donworth
Page 2
February 14, 19XX

1. Set up an electronic filing system and train all
   employees to use it to decrease the need for paper
   distribution in your office.

2. Purchase office supplies that come in nonplastic
   containers.

3. Encourage employees to bring or purchase lunches that
   do not come in plastic containers. Better yet,
   encourage employees to purchase inexpensive reusable
   containers to carry lunches.

4. Encourage employees to drink beverages in reusable
   containers or in aluminum or cardboard containers,
   which recycle more easily than plastic.

5. Encourage employees to place both hard and soft plastic
   in recycling bins. Many people are not aware that
   plastic is recyclable.

Our next pickup is scheduled for March 1. Please call me
directly at (913) 555-8987 if I can help in any way.

Sincerely,

Katherine Ross
Fund-Raising Specialist

jjk/midwest.ltr

1003 | Letter Parts

The parts of standard business letters may be categorized as required or optional. Required parts include information needed in any letter, regardless of the style. Optional parts include information needed with particular letter styles or in particular situations. For any of the letter parts listed below, see the section number in parentheses for more information:

Required Parts	*Optional Parts*
Return address (1004)	Attention line (1007)
Date (1005)	Complimentary close (1011)
Inside address (1006)	Company name (signature
Salutation/subject line	block) (1012)
(1008/1009)	Reference initials (1013)
Body (1010)	Filename (1013)
Writer's name (1012)	Enclosure notation (1014)
	Copy notation (1015)
	Postscript (1016)

1004 | Return Address

Placement of the return address depends on whether or not the letter is printed on letterhead. If you are using letterhead containing the return address, begin keying the date at about line 13 (or 2") (see figure 10.1). If you are not using letterhead containing the return address, begin keying the date at about line 6 (or 1") and place the return address at the end of the signature block (see figure 10.4). You may also, however, place the return address above the date, beginning at about line 6. In all cases, adjust the vertical placement of the letter when it is fully keyed (*see section 1002b, page 259*) and include the sender's complete address:

- Company name
- Street address
- City, state, and ZIP Code
- Telephone number (if not using letterhead that includes telephone number)

Date Line 1005

Include the month, day, and year with no abbreviations. See figures 10.1, 10.2, and 10.3 for placement of date line with block, modified-block, and simplified letter styles.

See section 602, page 148, and figure 10.9, page 278, for information on using the military and foreign correspondence date style.

> You can add the date to a letter quickly and accurately by using the Automatic Date feature of your software. Simply position your cursor where you wish the date to begin and enter the appropriate command. *Tech Tip*

Inside Address 1006

Generally, use capital and lowercase letters. However, use all capital letters for bulk mailings generated with a database in which the database address is used to address both the letter and the envelope (*see appendix C*). In either case, include the following:

- Addressee's name and title
- Company name
- Street address
- City, state, and ZIP Code

See figure 10.1 for placement of inside address.

See appendix C, figure C.2, for examples of addresses including post office boxes, building names and numbers, and regions of cities and for addresses to foreign countries.

a. Name and Title of Person Addressed. Always try to address a business letter to an individual within the organization. Include a courtesy, academic, or professional title *before* the name and the individual's job title, if known, *after* the name:

Courtesy Titles. Generally, use a courtesy title (e.g., *Mr., Ms.*) both in the inside address and on the envelope, except in the following instances:

- Omit the courtesy title when the first name could belong to either a male or female (e.g., *Leslie, Lee*) and you do not know the person's gender.
- Use *Ms.* when the addressee is female and her title preference is not known (*see section 901, page 223*).
- Omit courtesy titles, if you wish, when sending bulk mailings for which databases create mailing labels.

See figure 10.6, page 271, and section 702b, page 163, for more information on using courtesy titles. See section 1012, page 273, for information on using courtesy titles in signature blocks.

Job Titles. Include the title, if known, and place it either immediately after the name (separated by a comma) or on the next line, whichever placement creates a balanced appearance:

Ms. Mae Al-Jamal, Manager
Easter Aeronautics Inc.
7780 Executive Plaza
Kennebunkport, ME 04046

Ms. Miriam Yong
Director of Marketing
Oriental Exports Company
P.O. Box 1150
Stockton, CA 95201

Academic, Religious, and Government Titles.

See sections 503, page 139, and 703, page 164, for information on using these titles.

Addressee's Name Unknown. If you do not know the name of the person who should receive your letter, you may use a title instead:

Director of Sales
ABC Software Corporation
3876 South Shore Drive
Oklahoma City, OK 73105

See figures 10.2, 10.3, and 10.4 for situations in which an individual addressee's name is not known or when addressing a group of people.

More Than One Addressee. To save space, you may omit job titles.

See figure 10.9 for an example of a letter written to more than one person at the same address. See figure 10.5 for an example of a letter written to more than one person at different addresses.

b. Organization Names. Key organization names exactly as they appear in the organization's letterhead. When letterhead is not available, follow these guidelines:

- Abbreviate *Inc.* and *Ltd.*; do not abbreviate *Company* or *Corporation* unless the name is long and spelling these words out creates an unbalanced appearance.
- Do not use a comma before *Inc.* or *Ltd.*
- Capitalize all major words of the organization name. Do not capitalize prepositions or articles unless they are the first word in the organization name.

c. Street Address.

See sections 416b, page 82, and 704b, page 167, for information on using commas with and abbreviating words such as *Inc.*

Street Names. Spell out street names, including the ordinal numbers *first* through *tenth*. Use figures plus an ordinal designation (*th, st, rd,* or *nd*) for streets numbered *11th* and above.

See section 607e, page 155, for information on using ordinal numbers.

Street Designations and Compass Directions. Spell out and capitalize street designations (e.g., *Street*, *Boulevard*) and compass directions (e.g., *East*, *West*). However, when merging inside addresses from databases, limited database field space may require you to abbreviate such words. In this case, spell and abbreviate consistently within a document (and from document to envelope) by either spelling out street designations and compass directions or abbreviating both:

8990 East Lincoln Avenue   8990 E. Lincoln Ave.

45 Oak Street   45 Oak St.

Note: Postal Service guidelines recommend keying an address in all capital letters, using street and compass abbreviations with no punctuation. *See appendix C for a list of common street abbreviations and for complete guidelines on addressing envelopes.*

Building Names and Numbers. If a building name is part of the address, key it on the line above the street address:

Essex Plaza, Suite 125
2125 Duluth Boulevard

Note: Do not use the # symbol and the abbreviation *No.* after the word *suite* or *room*. Also, if an address includes several organizational levels, place them in order from the smallest to the largest:

Ms. Sara Ito, Chair
Linguistics Department
College of Liberal Arts
University of Texas
256 South Erie Street
Austin, TX 09876-1111

Post Office Boxes. If the address contains a post office box, place it on a separate line below the street address:

> 5566 Windsor Court
> P.O. Box 2201

d. City, State, and ZIP Code. Key full city name, two-letter state abbreviation (*see section 705, page 167*), and ZIP Code on the same line immediately below the street address (or post office box).

See appendix C for more information on addresses and ZIP Codes.

City Names. Abbreviate parts of city names (e.g., *Saint, Fort, Port*) only if they generally appear abbreviated:

> St. Paul, MN   Fort Knox, KY

State Abbreviations. Always use the two-letter state abbreviations, keyed in all capital letters with no space and no punctuation. (*See section 705a, page 167, for a list of the state abbreviations.*)

ZIP Codes. Use the ZIP+4 Code, if known. Key the ZIP Code two spaces after the state abbreviation:

> Livonia, MI 48152   Wilmore, KY 40390

Attention Line 1007

Use the attention line when you want a specific person to receive a letter whose message is intended for an entire company or group within the company. The attention line appears as the first line of the inside address and may include a person's name or simply a job title or department name (see figure 10.8 for format and placement):

> Attention Director of Sales
> Attention Personnel Department
> Attention Jon Walsh

Salutation

The salutation names the person, people, or organization addressed. When addressing an organization or group or when using an attention line (*see section 1007, page 269*), you may use phrases such as *Dear Colleagues* and *Dear Managers*. However, a better choice is the simplified letter style (see figure 10.3), which employs a subject line instead of a salutation (*see section 1009, page 272*).

See figure 10.1 for placement and format information. See figure 10.6 for common salutations.

See section 430, page 101, for information on using colons after salutations. See section 702b, page 163, for information on forming plurals of courtesy titles. See section 901, page 223, for a discussion of *Miss/Mrs./Ms.*

Addressee	Addressee and Salutation
Organization or group	Data Processing Managers Association Dear Colleagues: (or another group title) *or* Use simplified letter style with attention line and no salutation
Individual: Name known, gender unknown	Leslie Stark, President Dear Leslie Stark:
Individual: Name unknown, gender unknown	Purchasing Manager Dear Manager: (or another generic title)
Individual woman: Title preference unknown	Ms. Megan Flaten Dear Ms. Flaten:
Two or more individuals: Title preference known	Mr. Bill Roberts Mr. George Currie Dear Mr. Roberts and Mr. Currie: Ms. Lantha Cole Miss Joan Patterson Dear Ms. Cole and Miss Patterson: Miss Jill Kostner Miss Suzuko Danforth Dear Misses Kostner and Danforth:
Married couples: Traditional	Mr. and Mrs. Sinclair White Dear Mr. and Mrs. White:
Informal	Carlos and Maria Sanchez Dear Carlos and Maria:
One spouse has formal title	Senator Martha Grimes Mr. Hubert Grimes Dear Senator Grimes and Mr. Grimes:
Both spouses have formal title	Dr. Walter Johns Professor Kaye Johns Dear Dr. Johns and Professor Johns:
One spouse retains single name	Mr. Terry Melchewitz Ms. Ramona Johnson Dear Mr. Melchewitz and Ms. Johnson:
One spouse hyphenates name	Mr. W. Adams and Mrs. J. Mitchell-Adams Dear Mr. Adams and Mrs. Mitchell-Adams:

Fig. 10.6. Commonly used name forms for inside addresses and salutations.

1009 Subject (or Reference) Line

An all-caps subject line replaces the salutation in the simplified letter style (*see section 1001c, page 255, and figure 10.3*). A subject line or reference line also may be used with a salutation in block-style or modified block-style letters (two lines below the salutation) to indicate the topic or purpose of the letter (see figure 10.8).

Note: Some companies use a *When replying, refer to* line instead of a reference line to specify the topic, for example, an invoice or a file number. If this notation does not appear in the letterhead, key it two lines below the date (see figure 10.2).

1010 Body (Message) of Letter

Begin keying the body two lines below the salutation or subject line (three lines below in letters using a simplified style). See figure 10.1 for placement of the body within a letter. Format the following types of text as suggested below:

- Indented text (see figure 10.9) is generally indented one tab stop from the left margin. Lists (see figure 10.8) and numbered paragraphs (see figure 10.5) may be indented or aligned with the left margin.
- Tables are generally centered. Wider tables may be extended to reach left and right margins. See figure 10.5.
- Multiple-page letters require a special heading at the beginning of the second and subsequent pages (*see section 1002d, page 260, and figure 10.5*).

See section 1035, page 309, for information on creating tables. See sections 822–831, pages 195–198, for information on word division at the ends of lines in business letters.

Use the Indent (or Double Indent) feature of your software to format tabulated text and numbered paragraphs. This feature will indent one tab stop from the left margin (or from each margin) each time it is accessed.

Place the complimentary close two lines after the last line of the body, capitalizing only the first letter of the first word. Complimentary closings vary in formality. Figure 10.7 lists these variations. See figures 10.1 and 10.2 for format and placement of complimentary close with block and modified letter styles.

Level of Formality	Closing
Least formal; more personal (used for general business correspondence)	Sincerely, Sincerely yours, Cordially, Cordially yours, Yours sincerely,
More formal	Yours truly,
Most formal	Respectfully yours, Very truly yours,

Fig. 10.7. Commonly used complimentary closings.

Note: Occasionally, you may want to substitute a whole sentence for a closing in an informal letter (for example, *See you at the conference!* or *Let's get together next week*). In this case, punctuate the sentence normally and place it where the complimentary closing usually appears.

Many writers use the same closing in all letters. Since the name, title, and reference initials do not change, creating a *macro, (see section 902, page 243)* for the signature block and retrieving it as needed is an excellent timesaver. Simply add the filename after the reference initials.

Tech Tip

See section 501e, page 133, for information on capitalization in complimentary closings.

Writer's Name and Title (Signature Block) 1012

The writer's name appears four line spaces below the complimentary close (*see section 1011 above*). You may key the writer's title on the same line as the name (separated by a comma) or one line below the name, whichever creates a more balanced appearance:

Sincerely yours,   Yours truly,

J.T. Cox, Manager   Ivan H. Klutsinsky
                                    Controller

a. Courtesy Titles. Generally, do not include the writer's courtesy title (e.g., *Mr.*, *Ms.*) in the signature block, except in the following instances:

■ People whose names could be either male or female should include their preferred courtesy title in the keyed signature to avoid confusion:

Mr. Lynn Bates   Ms. Kelsey Moran   Mr. Morgan Lee

■ A writer who has a special title or a courtesy title preference should include this in the signature block. Though they may appear in the signature block, courtesy title preferences are generally not part of the handwritten signature:

Arthur A. Schultz, M.D.   Miss Anne Faxton
                            Director of Accounting

See section 1006a, page 265, for information on courtesy titles in inside addresses. See section 702b, page 163, for more information on using courtesy titles.

b. Department or Division Name. Department or division names should be keyed on the line below the writer's name:

Nanette F. O'Hare
Customer Services

See figure 10.1 for placement of writer's name, title, and department or division.

c. When One Person Signs for Another. When one person signs a letter for the sender, that person signs the sender's name and places his or her own initials after the signature; the signature and initials are often separated by a slash (/). See figure 10.9.

Reference Initials/Filename

1013

This notation includes the initials of the person who keyed the document (when not the writer) and the electronic filename (when the document is filed electronically). The filename allows the file to be retrieved quickly for editing or reference. See figure 10.1 for format and placement.

Enclosure Notation

1014

The word *enclosure*, usually abbreviated two lines below the reference initials (if used) or the signature block, indicates that materials are being sent with the letter (see figure 10.8 for format and placement). Several variations are acceptable, including those listed below:

Single Item Enclosed	*Multiple Items Enclosed*
Enclosure	Enclosures (2)
Enc	Enclosures 2
Attachment	Enc. 2
Invoice/check enclosed	Attachments
	Enclosures:
	1. Invoice 290
	2. Billing report
	3. Check

Note: If you want to send materials separately from the letter, key the notation *In a separate mailing* below the reference initials or enclosure notation, whichever is the last line. If there are several items, you may list them under the notation:

In a separate mailing:

1. Design specifications
2. Architect's drawings
3. Project cost estimates

| 1015 | **Copy Notation** |

The copy notation (e.g., *c M. Klein*) is used to tell the addressee which other people are receiving copies of the letter and to remind the sender to supply the copies (see figure 10.8). When copies are sent to several people, omit all titles and alphabetize the list (see figure 10.9). If you do not wish to have the addressee know that a particular individual is receiving a copy, use the blind copy notation, *bc*. This notation appears (handwritten or keyed) only on the single copy involved and the sender's file copy and is placed in the upper left corner of the page or at the bottom of the copy list (see figure 10.9).

| 1016 | **Postscripts** |

Postscripts express an aside, an afterthought, or a personal note such as *Happy Birthday*, *Congratulations,* or *Thanks for dinner* (see figure 10.8 for placement). The *PS* lead-in is optional. When it is used, it is followed by a colon.

Do not use postscripts to include information that should appear in the body of the letter; instead, revise and reprint the letter.

≡Rapid Postal Service   15 South State Street • Detroit, MI 59111-0333 • (777) 555-7878 Fax (777) 555-7898

November 15, 19XX

Attention line   Attention Communications Coordinator
First Interstate R\Trust Company
6567 Fostoria Avenue
Wichita, KS   67207

Dear Colleagues:

OPTIONAL FEATURES OF BUSINESS LETTERS   **Subject/reference line**

At our client's suggestion, we have prepared this letter
illustrating the recommended use, placement, and formatting of
optional features of business letters. We have also enclosed
a brochure on U.S. Postal Service guidelines.

Note that indented text is positioned one tab stop from the
left margin; use the Indent feature of your software, if you
wish. Note also the placement of these parts:

Indented text
          * Attention line
          * Subject line
          * Indented text
          * Delivery notation
          * Enclosure notation
          * Copy notation
          * Postscript

If I can help in any other way, please call.

Sincerely,

Jeannette Brownson
Public Relations Specialist

**Reference
initials/filename** yrt/optparts.let

          Enc   **Enclosure notation**

Copy notation c M. Patterson

Delivery notation By registered mail

Postscript   Don't forget to reserve space at the upcoming seminar, "You
and Your Words." Just call (313) 565-7800 today.

**Fig. 10.8. Block-style letter (recommended style) showing
placement and formatting of optional letter parts.**

COMMUNICATIONS INC.

15 November 19XX

Ms. Gretchen Helmut, Vice President
Mr. Otto Schmidt, Personnel Manager
Bonn Corporation
57 Oststrasse
Munich 3500
GERMANY

Dear Ms. Helmut and Mr. Schmidt:

Enclosed is the final report of the market analysis we conducted
in your area. Based on this information and our discussion with
your representatives, we recommend that you select one employee
from each department for training in your Language and Culture
Program. Here, briefly, is our rationale:

Although many of your employees already speak
English, French, and Italian, your company does over
one-third of its business in South America, China,
and Southeast Asia. This suggests that you and your
business partners in these countries would benefit if
your company had representatives fluent in Spanish,
Portugese, Chinese, Japanese, and Korean.

The attached report provides our findings, rationale, and
specific recommendations. We will contact you soon to arrange
a follow-up meeting.

Sincerely,

Althea Gordon /ptr

Althea Gordon
Research Specialist

ptr/bonn.let

Enc

c   S. Creger
     J. Little
     T. Hedin

bc V. Roeser

**Fig. 10.9. Block-style international letter showing
selected optional letter parts.**

International Correspondence

1017

With the increased number of firms conducting business worldwide, international written communication has assumed a new importance. Follow these guidelines when corresponding internationally, especially with people for whom English is not the primary language:

- Use a direct writing style and clear, precise words. Those who speak English as a second language are generally not familiar with English slang, jargon, and idioms.
- Develop an awareness of cultural differences that may interfere with the communication process.

See section 203k, page 26, for information on eliminating bias from your writing.

Formatting International Correspondence

1018

Except for minor differences in formatting inside addresses (*see figure 10.9 and section 1006, page 265*) and dates (*see section 602, page 148*), prepare correspondence to foreign readers as you would to any other reader. Research suggests that many correspondents from other countries use the modified-block style letter. In addition, business people from other countries tend to write in a more formal tone. You may wish to model your return correspondence on the styles you observe.

International Addresses

1019

Use the company's letterhead or a business card as a guide for spelling and other information. Include the following:

- Addressee's Name, Title
- Company Name
- Street Address
- City and Codes
- COUNTRY NAME (capitalized)

See figure 10.9 and appendix C, figure C.2, for more information on addresses outside the United States.

1020 | **Canadian Codes and Province Abbreviations**

When addressing mail to most countries, you need to key the country's name as the last line. However, Canada uses a coding system called the *National Postal Code*, which may be placed on the city and province line or with the country name on the last line of the envelope address (*see appendix C for envelope formats*). Use the following two-letter abbreviations for provinces:

AB	Alberta	NT	Northwest Territories
BC	British Columbia	ON	Ontario
LB	Labrador	PE	Prince Edward Island
MB	Manitoba	PQ	Quebec
NB	New Brunswick	SK	Saskatchewan
NS	Nova Scotia	YT	Yukon Territory

1021 | **Envelopes**

The information in the envelope's mailing address should match the information in the inside address. The format of envelope addresses should be consistent with current U.S. Postal Service guidelines, which recommend all capital letters and no punctuation (*see appendix C*). However, if your company uses the traditional format (upper- and lowercase), follow your company's preference.

INTEROFFICE MEMORANDUMS

Interoffice memorandums (usually called *memos*) are used to communicate within an organization. All the principles of business letter writing apply, but memos tend to be more direct and informal than letters.

Margins 1022

Generally, use your word processor's 1" defaults for the top, bottom, left, and right margins. Make the necessary spacing adjustments for very short or very long memos (*see section 1002d, page 260*). If you are using preprinted memo forms, align the left margin of your text with the memo headings.

Justification 1023

As with business letters, use left justification rather than full justification to make reading easier.

Simplified Memo Format 1024

Memo formats vary greatly from one organization to another. If your organization has an established format, use it. If not, use the simplified format shown in figure 10.10. Note the formatting of the memo's heading information:

a. Title. If you are using plain paper, key the word MEMORANDUM in all capital letters, centered, on line 1 or 1" from the top of the page. If you are using letterhead, key MEMORANDUM, centered, three lines below the last line of the letterhead.

b. Date. Key the full date with no abbreviations.

c. TO Line. This may simply refer to the distribution list (names appear at the end of the memo) or to individuals. If you list individuals' names, include a title or department below or beside each name. Do not use courtesy titles.

d. Sender. Include the sender's job title or department below or beside the name. The sender should initial his or her keyed name before delivering the memo.

e. Subject Line. The subject line should describe the memo's contents accurately and concisely. Key the subject line in all capital letters.

f. Body. Begin keying the body three lines below the subject line. Use single spacing with double spacing between paragraphs.

g. Reference Initials/Filename. As on business letters, reference initials are those of the person keying the memo, if not the writer. The filename, used for electronically stored documents, helps workers find the document for reference or editing.

h. Attachment Notation. With memos, the word *Attachment* is frequently used instead of *Enclosure* to alert readers that materials accompany the memo.

i. Distribution List. Use this list when the memo is sent to several people. Order the list alphabetically.

Note: Memos longer than one page use the same continuation page heading as a multiple-page letter (see figure 10.5).

See section 1028, page 289, and figure 10.16 for information on memo reports. See sections 205–206, page 28, for information on proofreading documents and on proofreaders' marks.

```
                    MEMORANDUM                          1-inch top and bottom
                                                        margins

October 25, 19XX    2 returns                           Heading (centered)

                                                        Date line
TO:  Distribution List   2 returns
                                                        Receiver
Marshall Kinzer
Office Manager   2 returns                              Sender

MEMO FORMAT    3 returns                                Subject line


The NASOA Office Support Staff Task Force has completed its  Left
assignment to develop standardized forms for companywide     justification
use.  This memo and those attached illustrate the newly       (ragged right)
adopted format for memorandums.

All but one of the traditional guide words are no longer
needed. However, double spacing is maintained between the
sections of heading information.  The body begins on the
third line after the capitalized subject line.              1-inch left and right
                                                            margins
Key lists of information as follows:

    *  Use an asterisk, bullet, number, or letter to introduce
       each item.
    *  Single-space within lists, but double-space above and
       below lists.
    *  Indent lists one tab stop from the left margin.

When a memo is being sent to more than one person, include
an alphabetical distribution list after the end references
(reference initials and attachment notations).

After the reference initials, include a filename to ensure
easy file retrieval.
                                                            Reference
erw/format.mem                                              initials/filename

Attachment                                                 Attachment notation

Distribution:                                              Distribution list
A. Andreisen                                               (alphabetical)
S. Calver
K. Mai
```

Fig. 10.10. Simplified memo format.

Many companies prefer using the traditional memo format of four headings on either plain paper or preprinted memo forms (see second example below). The traditional format differs from the simplified format (*see section 1024, page 281*) only in the heading structure. Several variations exist. Below are two versions of the traditional heading structure, one in which headings align at the left margin and one in which headings align at the colons:

```
DATE:      April 12, 19XX

TO:        Don Recker, Marketing Department

FROM:      Mary Winslow, Marketing Consultant

SUBJECT:   MARKETING PLAN FOR NEW PRODUCT LINE
```

KEY INDUSTRIES

MEMORANDUM

```
   DATE:   April 12, 19XX

     TO:   Don Recker, Marketing Department

   FROM:   Mary Winslow, Marketing Consultant

SUBJECT:   MARKETING PLAN FOR NEW PRODUCT LINE
```

Tech Tip When using printed memo forms with the traditional format, set up a *macro* (*see section 902, page 243*) for filling in the heading information. For plain paper memos, create a file containing the title *Memorandum* and headings.

Many organizations prepare written agendas for their meetings and record highlights of their meetings with written minutes (notes). The format of agendas and minutes varies from highly structured notes to a simple listing of topics for discussion. The guidelines presented below follow the traditional model for organizational minutes. If your company or organization requires formal agendas and minutes based on standard parliamentary procedure, consult a guide to parliamentary procedure (*see appendix E*).

Agendas 1026

Agendas outline a meeting's order of business. Participants normally receive an agenda before the meeting begins. Like the informal sample agenda presented (figure 10.11), most agendas contain the following information:

a. Heading. Include the name of the group, the date of the meeting, and, if possible, the purpose of the meeting.

b. Order of Business. List meeting topics in order of discussion. Begin with a *call to order* stating the time the meeting will begin.

Approval of Minutes. Standing groups—groups that meet regularly to make decisions affecting a specific operational area—must often approve minutes of their previous meeting before discussing new items. Thus, the *approval of minutes* often appears after the *call to order*.

Approval of Treasurer's Report. If the group manages its own budget, collecting and disbursing its funds, the group's treasurer often speaks at each meeting, reporting budget balances, recent spending, and anticipated expenses. This agenda item should appear after the *approval of minutes*.

Old Business.   Generally, groups finish discussions from previous meetings or report on previous decisions before discussing new items. Thus, *old business* usually appears as an agenda item with as many subtopics as necessary.

New Business.   Usually the main focus of the meeting, *new business* includes as many subtopics as necessary. The last of these subtopics is often *other* to include any discussion items not anticipated by the person writing the agenda.

Adjournment.   Include the time at which the meeting will end, allowing participants to plan their other activities accordingly.

```
                                                          1-inch top
                                                          margin

        MEETING OF THE HUMAN RESOURCES EXECUTIVE COMMITTEE   Name of group

                     September 1, 19XX                    Meeting date

                          AGENDA                          Title

    1. Call to order:  9:00 a.m.                          Meeting topics
                                                          in order of
    2. Approval of minutes from August 2 meeting.         discussion

    3. Old business:

          a. Report of preliminary findings of the computer   1-inch left and
             usage task force.                             right margins
          b. Report on current service contracts.
          c. Report on personnel actions in August.

    4. New business:

          a. Anticipated personnel action in September.
          b. Management-labor negotiation plan.
          c. Other.

    5. Adjournment:  10:30 a.m.
```

Fig. 10.11. Traditional organizational meeting agenda.

Preparing informative meeting minutes begins with taking accurate notes on the discussion. Minutes range from informal notes to formal corporate minutes, depending on the organization, the group's preference, the purpose of the meeting, and the purpose of the minutes. Figure 10.12 presents an example of informal minutes, including the following:

a. Heading. Include the group's name, the date of the meeting, and, if possible, the purpose of the meeting.

b. Topic Headings. Organize information clearly to correspond to the agenda. Use headings that allow readers to locate information easily.

c. Content of Minutes. Minutes should be concise and selective. Recorders should avoid transcribing discussion or even summarizing major points of discussion or debate. Instead, they should limit their minutes to recording the following:

- Summaries of reports
- Decisions made
- Actions taken

d. Signature of Recorder. Include or omit, according to your organization's practice.

```
                MEETING OF THE HUMAN RESOURCES EXECUTIVE COMMITTEE
```

Meeting date   September 1, 19XX

```
                                    MINUTES
```

Topic   APPROVAL OF   Minutes of the August 2 meeting were approved.
headings MINUTES   Tom Seiko noted that the correct dates of the
                          national meeting are December 15-17.

Discussion COMPUTER TASK   The task force reported its initial findings.
summary FORCE   The committee agreed that more data is needed.
                          The task force will present its final report
                          at the November meeting.

          SERVICE   The following service contracts are scheduled
          CONTRACTS   for renewal on January 1:   Office Cleaners
                          Inc., PQT Stationers, and R.J. Smith Services.
                          The committee approved renewing each at an
                          increased price not to exceed 10 percent.

          PERSONNEL   The resignation of Diana Curry, receptionist,
          ACTIONS   was accepted.

          NEW BUSINESS   Applicants for the receptionist job are being
                          interviewed now.   The position should be
                          filled within two weeks.

                          A report outlining plans for forthcoming
                          negotiations with the support staff union was
                          accepted and is attached.

          ADJOURNMENT   10:25 a.m.

Fig. 10.12. Typical informal minutes.

Business reports are typically multiple-page, informative documents written for a specific purpose: to analyze data, to present a proposal, to report on activities, to discuss various solutions to a problem, and so on. Report formats vary widely among organizations; thus, no comprehensive business reporting source is available. General guidelines are provided here; however, if your organization uses a report format that differs from the guidelines in this section, use your company's format. Whatever formatting options you choose, be certain they are consistent throughout the document.

Types of Business Reports   1028

Business reports range from informal to formal:

a. Formal Reports. Formal (and longer) reports generally consist of three major parts: front matter, body, and end matter. Each of these three parts consists of subparts (*see sections 1029–1031, pages 289–297*).

b. Informal Reports. Informal reports often appear in memo form (*see sections 1021–1022, pages 280–281*) and are, therefore, called *memo reports*. Because of their brevity, memo reports usually do not include front matter or end matter. However, their bodies generally consist of six sections, each with a specific purpose (*see section 1030, page 294, and figure 10.16*).

Front Matter   1029

The front matter of a formal report is anything that precedes the body. Front matter typically includes the following parts:

- Letter of transmittal
- Cover or title page
- Table of contents
- List of tables or figures
- Preface

a. Letter of Transmittal. The letter of transmittal observes all the formatting guidelines for other business letters. Because it introduces the report to the reader, it should be attached to the front of the document.

b. Cover or Title Page. Long formal reports typically include as the first page a title page, which lists the title and subtitle (if appropriate), the writer, the readers (group), and the date submitted. Arrange the information to achieve a pleasing visual balance. See figure 10.13.

Use the Center Page feature of your software to center the title page text.

c. Table of Contents. The table of contents lists the report's major sections and their page numbers. Prepare the table of contents last so that all page numbers are present and accurate. In addition, use leaders (spaced periods) to help the reader's eye move from section titles to page numbers. See figure 10.14.

If your word processor has an automatic Table of Contents feature, use it. Some word processing packages have a feature that creates automatic leaders.

```
ERGONOMIC IMPLICATIONS FOR THE INSTALLATION
    OF INFORMATION PROCESSING SYSTEMS
         AT DOCKSIDE CORPORATION




                Prepared by

           Office Ergonomics Inc.




                Submitted to

           Dockside Corporation
             Earl J. VanDeven
       Information Processing Specialist


              August 1, 19XX
```

Fig. 10.13. Sample report title page.

```
                    TABLE OF CONTENTS


                                              Page


LIST OF TABLES  .  .  .  .  .  .  .  .  .  .  . .  iii

    PREFACE  .  .  .  .  .  .  .  .  .  .  .  .  .  iv

    SUMMARY  .  .  .  .  .  .  .  .  .  .  .  .  .  1

    BACKGROUND  .  .  .  .  .  .  .  .  .  .  .  .  2

        Situation  .  .  .  .  .  .  .  .  .  .  2

        Problem Statement  .  .  .  .  .  .  .  .  4

    FINDINGS  .  .  .  .  .  .  .  .  .  .  .  .  5

        Regional Prospects  .  .  .  .  .  .  .  .  6

        National Prospects  .  .  .  .  .  .  .  7

        International Prospects  .  .  .  .  .  .  8

    CONCLUSION  .  .  .  .  .  .  .  .  .  .  .  9

    RECOMMENDATIONS  .  .  .  .  .  .  .  .  .  .  10

    FOLLOW-UP  .  .  .  .  .  .  .  .  .  .  .  .  11

WORKS CITED  .  .  .  .  .  .  .  .  .  .  .  .  12

APPENDIX  .  .  .  .  .  .  .  .  .  .  .  .  .  13

                        ii
```

Fig. 10.14. Sample table of contents.

d. Lists of Tables and Figures. When the report contains several tables or figures, create a list of them and place it after the table of contents. In addition, include figure or table titles, numbers, and page numbers in the table of contents. See figure 10.15.

Number all tables and figures in your report; number them consecutively throughout the report or within each chapter or section. When numbered separately in each section, the figure's section number should precede the figure number. For example, *Table 2–1* refers to the first table that appears in section 2. *Table 2–3* refers to the third table that appears in section 2.

```
                         LIST OF FIGURES

    Figure                                               Page


    1. Average Annual Pay Increase Per Level of Employment . . . 3

    2. Percent of Budget Spent on Salaries and Other Items . . 7

    3. Average Salary Compared with Competitors' . . . . . . . .12

    4. Average Annual Pay Increase within Departments . . . .19

    5. Increase in Percent of Budget Spent on Benefits . . . .22
```

Fig. 10.15. List of figures.

e. Preface. Also known as a *foreword*, the preface is an optional part of the report used to convey a special message to the reader, such as additional—but never essential—information about the report. Place it before the table of contents or immediately before the body of the report.

Many writers develop the body of a business report first because it determines the other parts of the report. The amount and complexity of the information in the report will, of course, determine the length of the body; however, both long and short business reports present information using a similar organizational structure, including six separately headed parts. Figure 10.16 illustrates the following six parts within a memo report, but the same parts generally appear in longer, more formal business reports as well:

a. Summary. Sometimes called the *executive summary*, this section presents a short synopsis of the entire report, drawing information from each section that follows. The length of the summary will vary in proportion to the length of the report, usually between one paragraph and one page. See figure 10.16.

b. Background. The background section describes the circumstances or information that led to the report and, in doing so, states the purpose of the report as well. See figure 10.16.

c. Findings. Business people base many of their decisions on the strength of supporting data presented in the findings section of a report. Data often appears both textually and graphically, with text interpreting and highlighting the graphics. See figure 10.16.

See section 1035, page 309, for information on creating tables and figure 10.5 for an example of a table used in text.

d. Conclusion. The conclusion relates the findings to the report's purpose. See figure 10.16.

e. Recommendations. This section recommends action based on the conclusion. See figure 10.16.

f. Follow-Up. This section states the ways in which the writer intends to act on the report's recommendations. Specific follow-up activities may include seeking permission to change a policy, implementing a new procedure, or requesting funding to gather more data. See figure 10.16.

See section 1033f, page 305, for information on headings used to set off text.

June 10, 19XX

TO: Bonita Legeros

Sharon Hill

MEMORANDUM REPORT PREPARATION

Reports in business are frequently prepared in different forms from those in education. You are looking at a very popular example, the memo report. Rather than prepare both a report and an accompanying letter or memo, the two are combined. This method is usually used for reports that are fairly short, fewer than three pages.

Many times you will find that the report content lends itself to the use of subheadings as shown below.

Summary

Summary. The findings of the survey of advertising at Old London Square Mall are similar to the national trends. All the mall stores use, in addition to local cooperative advertising, some type of outside media. The choice of outside media compares quite closely with national trends, since newspapers are listed most effective and used most frequently, followed by radio, television, direct mailing, and magazines.

Background

Background. Our organization entered into an agreement three months ago with the merchants of the Old London Square Mall to investigate avenues of approach to effective advertising. We assigned methods currently in use throughout the nation, and especially those methods utilized by businesses in some type of physical-location arrangement (shopping centers, malls, and so on). After gathering the evidence used throughout the country, we prepared a questionnaire and administered it to all the merchants located in the Old London Square Mall. The results of both the nationwide survey and the mall survey were then compared.

Figure 10.16. Memo report.

Legeros
Page 2
June 10, 19XX

Findings *Findings.* Nationwide, merchants agree that individual firms
must do more advertising. Cooperative efforts seem to be
quite effective when the entire mall conducts some type of
sale, but for the remainder of the time individual firms must
generate sales by individual advertising efforts. The Old
London Square Mall merchants agree with this 100%. The
national use of various types of advertising media differs
slightly from what the mall merchants now use.

Types of Advertising Media *

Nationwide	Old London Square Mall
Newspaper	Newspaper
Television	Radio
Radio	Television
Direct mail	Direct mail
Magazines	Magazines

* Ranked according to frequency of use

Conclusion *Conclusion.* The use of advertising media by merchants at the
Old London Square Mall closely follows what is being done on
a national scale. The only difference found was in the
ranking of television and radio. Television is second in
popularity nationwide, and radio is third. At this mall
radio is second, and television is third.

Recommendations. Our agreement called for both a written **Recommendations**
report and an oral presentation of the findings. This
information was given to the merchants at their last monthly
meeting. A recommendation was made that the merchants use
television more than radio in the future. It was decided to
follow this recommendation for the next six months, after
which a follow-up report will be prepared.

Follow-up *Follow-Up.* Jim Lane will be in charge of the follow-up
research project. Alice Barnes, June Folton, Bob Arterburn,
and Leslie Barth will work with him.

Figure 10.16. Memo report continued.

The end matter of business reports usually consists of endnotes (if necessary), a works-cited page, and appendixes:

a. Endnotes. Occasionally writers want to comment on information in their reports. They may also want their readers to have additional explanation, description, or support for ideas. Because this information may not be vital to the report's main points, writers include it at the end as an optional section. Information essential to the report should not be placed in an endnote, and endnotes are generally not used to cite information sources (*see section 1032, page 299*).

Endnotes should begin on a separate page immediately following the last page of the body of the report. The first-level heading *Notes* or *Endnotes* should begin the page (*see section 1033f, page 305, for more information on heading levels*). Also, if a single endnote exists, the writer may simply write "see note" in parentheses near the applicable text. However, if more than one endnote exists, a superscript number in the text alerts the reader to the corresponding note. Consider, for example, the sentence below, which includes a superscript number to indicate an endnote:

```
Since a large majority of students in any
institution of higher learning are legal adults,
but are often uncertain of their legal rights and
obligations (Largent 19), a study should be
conducted to investigate the feasibility of
employing a lawyer for the students.[1]
```

Use the Endnote feature, if available with your word processing program, to automatically create endnotes as you key a report.

Tech Tip

1. Largent also points out that many public school
   systems provide simple legal services for students
   but that lawyers function under severe
   limitations. First, they provide only minimal
   services, such as advice on handling small claims
   court actions and landlord disputes. Thus, when
   students need further assistance, including court
   appearances, these school systems lawyers can only
   refer them to others, who then charge for
   services. Second, public school-supplied lawyers
   often maintain private practice outside the school
   environment and are paid little for their service
   to schools. Thus, some students have questioned
   the real dedication of these lawyers to their
   nonpaying school clientele. In some cases,
   conflict of interest charges have arisen when
   lawyers, operating as advisors in the schools,
   have referred students to their own legal service
   or to a friend's service. For the purposes of
   this study, then, these part-time legal advisory
   services provided by schools are not considered
   legal services because of their limitations.

b. Works-Cited Page. The works-cited page at the end of the report lists each source from which the writer borrowed information. *See section 1032, page 299, for more information.*

See section 450, page 121, for information on underlining and italicizing titles.See section 439, page 109, for information on placing titles in quotation marks.

c. Appendixes. An appendix is a collection of information on a single topic that is not part of the central topic or argument of the report. Appendixes contain information that the reader may or may not want to read, such as additional statistics, historical data related to the topic of the report, lists of technical terms with definitions, and so on. The appendixes of this manual serve as good examples. Each of them is considered (and labeled) as a separate appendix and is given its own title. Each is also listed in the table of contents.

Citing Information Sources 1032

Report writers commonly borrow (i.e., quote, paraphrase, or summarize) information from other written or spoken sources. They must cite the sources of any such borrowed information, and various systems are available for doing so. Perhaps the most efficient system is promoted by the Modern Language Association (MLA) in its most recent edition of the *MLA Handbook for Writers of Research Papers*. The main points of this system appear briefly in sections 1032a-b; however, if you cite information sources frequently within your business reports, refer to the *MLA Handbook* for more detailed information.

The MLA system combines a works-cited list at the end of the report with brief text references to the works-cited list.

a. Works-Cited List. Appearing on its own page between the endnotes and the appendixes (*see section 1031b, page 298*), the works-cited list must provide full citations for all sources of borrowed information. Cite each source by presenting information in the following order:

1. Author(s), last name first
2. Title
3. Place of publication or presentation (books and speeches)

   Larger work published within (articles)
4. Date of publication or presentation
5. Pages (if part of larger work)

Examples of a typical book, speech, and article citation appear below. Note that a period separates the author(s) from the title and the title from the place of publication and the publication date:

Book

```
Bartholemew, J. Personal Law and You.  New York:
    Legal P, 1992.
```

Speech

```
Venduzi, C.  Keynote Address.  Twenty-fifth Annual
    Meeting of Midwest Lawyers. Chicago, Dec. 19-21,
    1991.
```

Article

```
Largent, R.L.   "Forgotten Customers."   American
    Legal Journal 9 (1991): 14-21.
```

Follow these additional guidelines for creating the works-cited list, all of which are illustrated in figure 10.17b:

- Use minimal information without sacrificing clarity. For example, use the author's first initials instead of names; omit state abbreviations when using well known city names; omit phrases such as *Publishing Company* in company names and use the abbreviation P to stand for the word *Press* in publishers' names.
- Place the first line of each citation at the left margin. Indent second and subsequent lines one tab stop. This allows readers to glance quickly down the left margin to find the sources they need.
- Alphabetize citations by their first entry, which is usually (but not always) the author's last name.
- Italicize (or underline) book, magazine, and journal titles. Place article and speech titles in quotation marks. Capitalize major words of titles.

b. Text References to Works-Cited List. With a works-cited list at the end of the report, writers can easily cite any borrowed information that appears in their text, often with only a single word and/or page number. Consider the following sentences, both of which effectively cite their source without using unnecessary information:

Option 1

Bartholemew believes that all institutions are "genuinely responsive to the essential problems but may be irrelevant to those problems if necessary legal services are not readily obtainable by those who might benefit from them" (212).

Option 2

All institutions are "genuinely responsive to the essential problems but may be irrelevant to those problems if necessary legal services are not readily obtainable by those who might benefit from them" (Bartholemew 212).

In the first option above, the writer cites the source by (1) mentioning the author's name in the text and (2) placing in parentheses the page number from which the information was borrowed. In the second option, the writer does not use the author's name in the text and must, therefore, do so in parentheses after the borrowed material.

In either case, since the full citation for the Bartholemew source appears on the works-cited page, the writer need not repeat it in a footnote. The author need only supply enough information to direct readers to the works-cited list. See figure 10.17 for information on formatting the works-cited list and referring to the list within the report.

See section 1031a, page 297, for information on using endnotes. See section 442b, page 112, for information on indenting long quotations. See section 437, page 106, for

University Student Services

We cannot consider this larger problem, however, without considering another side of the issue: whether it is even feasible to provide legal services to students.

First-level heading

THE FEASIBILITY OF PROVIDING STUDENT LEGAL SERVICES

Source cited by reference to author on work-cited list

Page number within source

There is a genuine concern of both lay people and legal professionals over the unavailability of needed legal services. Bartholemew believes that all institutions are "genuinely responsive to the essential problems but may be irrelevant to those problems if necessary legal services are not readily obtainable by those who might benefit from them" (212).

Second-level heading

The Problem

Since a large majority of students in any institution of higher learning are legal adults but are often uncertain of their legal rights and obligations (Largent 19), a study should be conducted to investigate the feasibility of employing a lawyer for the students.

Source cited by reference to author on work-cited list

Third-level heading

Statement of Problem. The purpose of this study will be to (1) determine the amount of need for legal services by students, (2) survey the desire for and attitudes toward this proposal by a representative sample of the student body and faculty, (3) discover the physical workability of such a program, and (4) determine what services should be provided.

Source cited by title and page number within source

Importance of Study. The article "Just When We Thought It Was Safe" notes a survey of 1,000 New York students. In a five-year period, 25% reported that they had encountered legal problems. Only 3.5% ever spoke to a lawyer, and just 1.1% retained counsel (13). This seems to be an indication that, although the need is present, few people receive the legal attention necessary for their problems. This same situation of inaccessibility is stated in yet another way in that the financially well-to-do are aware of their need for legal services and have no trouble obtaining them. The financially poor may be aware of their need but are unable to obtain legal services (Venduzi).

Oral source cited (no page number necessary)

4

Figure 10.17a. Page from report with flush-right running header, a centered main heading, a flush-left subheading, and a flush-left sub-subheading.

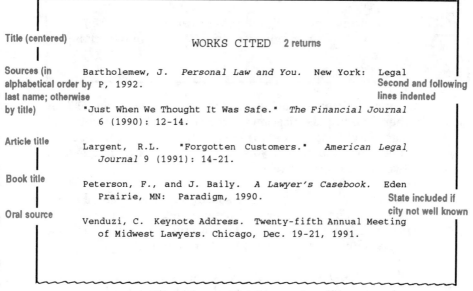

WORKS CITED   2 returns

Bartholemew, J.   *Personal Law and You.*   New York: Legal
P, 1992.

"Just When We Thought It Was Safe."   *The Financial Journal*
6 (1990): 12-14.

Largent, R.L.   "Forgotten Customers."   *American Legal*
Journal 9 (1991): 14-21.

Peterson, F., and J. Baily.   *A Lawyer's Casebook.*   Eden
Prairie, MN: Paradigm, 1990.

Venduzi, C. Keynote Address. Twenty-fifth Annual Meeting
of Midwest Lawyers. Chicago, Dec. 19-21, 1991.

Fig 10.17b. Works-cited page.

information on quoting other people's words. See section
445, page 116, for information on using ellipsis marks and
brackets to indicate omissions from and additions to
quotations.

Report Formatting | 1033 |

See sections 1002, page 259, and 1024, page 281, for
information on letter and memo formatting. See sections 205
and 206, page 28, for information on proofreading
documents and on proofreaders' marks.

a. Margins.   Generally, use 1" margins.   However, if your
report will be bound, change the left margin to 1.25" or 1.5" to
accommodate the binding.

The printer menu of your software may include a Binding feature. This eliminates the need for you to change margins.

b. Justification. To aid readability, use left justification rather than full justification for your report. Many people find a ragged right edge easier to read (see figure 10.17). If you must double-space the report, you need not add extra line spaces between headings and text.

c. Spacing. Generally, single-space your reports and double-space between paragraphs and between headings and text (see figure 10.17). If you must double-space the report, you need not add extra line spaces between headings and text.

d. Page Breaks. Inevitably, paragraphs will not all begin and end on the same page. However, do not leave a single line of a paragraph at the top or bottom of any given page. Also, when possible, avoid page breaks that separate blocks of text such as indented quotations, lists, tables, and other figures. See figure 10.5 for an example of a table used within text.

See sections 403 (page 69), 404 (page 70), 428b (page 99), and 501c (page 131) for information on formatting vertical lists.

Activate the Widow/Orphan Protect feature of your software to avoid leaving single lines at the bottom or top of any page. Also, use a Block Protect feature to keep page breaks from separating indented quotations, lists, tables, and other figures.

e. Page Numbering. Many page-numbering options exist. If your organization does not specify a system, do the following:

Number front-matter pages at the bottom with centered, lowercase Roman numerals (i.e., *i, ii, iii, iv*); count the title page as page *i*, but do not print the page number on it. See figure 10.14.

Number the body and end matter of your report continuously with Arabic numbers (i.e., *1, 2, 3*), with the number *1* appearing on the first page of text. When numbering pages at the top, place page numbers 1" from the top, with the first line of text .5" below the page number. When numbering pages at the bottom, the bottom margin may be decreased to .5". This will place the page number .5" from the bottom of the page and will place the last line of text 1" from the bottom of the page. See figure 10.17.

> The Page Numbering feature of your word processor numbers pages automatically. It will renumber pages whenever you insert or delete text and graphics. Another option is to include page numbers within a header or footer. *Tech Tip*

f. Headings. Use headings to help the reader see the organization of your report. Follow these guidelines:

Level 1 (Main Headings):	Flush left and ALL CAPITALIZED
Level 2 (Subheadings):	Flush left, separate from text, italicized
Level 3 (Sub-subheadings):	Flush left, run into text with period at end, italicized

Note: If you use only two heading levels in a report, you need not use the level 1 heading described above; you may choose to use the other two levels, making level 2 as described above your highest level heading. See figure 10.17. *See section 1030, page 294, for standard report parts that might be set off by headings.*

g. Headers and Footers. For longer reports, include a brief header or footer on each page to remind readers which section of the report they are reading. The section heading or title often serves as the header throughout the section. See figure 10.17.

h. Text Enhancements. While text enhancements such as boldfacing, underlining, and italicizing can effectively highlight text, these features lose their effect when overused. Use them selectively for maximum effect.

Also, most people find traditional Courier or Roman 10-point typefaces easiest to read; therefore, use them as the main typeface for your reports. As with other text enhancements, use typeface changes selectively to highlight and emphasize. Also, use all text enhancements consistently; that is, use the same enhancement for the same purpose throughout the report.

See sections 438, page 108, and 451, page 122, for information on using quotation marks and italics for emphasis.

| 1034 | **Outlining Business Documents**

Outlines display the organization of business reports and other complex documents. An outline represents the major divisions, secondary topics, and supporting data covered in a document. Writers may use outlines to help them organize their ideas before they write; they may also use outlines in the revision stage to help them analyze the organization of their document.

However, outlines may also serve as an aid to presentation. In some cases, writers or speakers formalize and submit outlines to supervisors, coworkers, readers, or listeners to show the division and organization of complex or lengthy information.

Figure 10.18 presents a brief sample outline, illustrating the following guidelines:

a. Section Designations. Use Roman numerals to identify major divisions and capital letters to identify secondary divisions. Use Arabic numbers to identify major points under secondary divisions, lowercase letters to identify minor points, and parentheses to indicate supporting data under minor points.

b. Alignment. Numbers and letters at equal levels should align vertically at the period.

c. Division Logic. Outlines represent an abbreviated way to show the organizational logic of a document. In an outline, each level is a *breakdown* of material governed by the topic heading of the next highest level. Thus, just as you would not use a I without a II, you should not use an A if you cannot include at least a B. This is true at all levels.

d. Parallel Structure. Describe entries within the same level using the same language structure; that is, entries within the same level should be parallel. For example, all entries at one level should begin with a noun or noun phrase, or they should all begin with a verb, or verb phrase.

See sections 402, page 68, and 501d, page 132, for information on using periods and capitalization in outlines. See section 203e, page 19, for more information on parallel structure.

Some word processing programs include an Outline feature that automatically numbers the different levels of text.

```
                    THE ADMINISTRATIVE MANAGER

Major division    I. Need

Secondary           A.  Business growth
division
                    B.  New employees and the administrative manager

                 II. Changes

                    A.  Rising financial costs

Major point            1.  Increased paperwork

                       2.  Inflation

Numbers and         B.  Employee changes
letters align at
periods                1.  Retirement

                       2.  Automation

                       3.  Insufficient training

Minor point               a.  New technology
Supporting data
                              (1)  Increased training needs

                              (2)  Decreased workforce needs

                          b.  Veteran workers
Parallel
grammatical         C.  Career options
construction in
entries (all are       1.  Strong need for administrative managers
nouns)
                       2.  Postsecondary school programs
```

Fig. 10.18. Outline.

Tables enhance text by presenting information in a graphic form and providing more information in less space. Table columns present information vertically (generally top to bottom) and table rows present information horizontally (generally left to right). Cells are junctures between columns and rows and usually provide information relating the column heading and the row heading. Figures 10.19 through 10.21 provide examples of tables illustrating the use of columns and rows as well as the following qualities relating to table format and page placement:

a. Table Format. Format tables to create a balanced, readable, and pleasing appearance on the page. Generally, the following guidelines are helpful:

- Name the table to reflect accurately the information presented. Capitalize all major title words.
- Create short, clear headings for columns and rows. Capitalize all major words. Column headings should be consistently flush left or centered. Row headings are usually flush left.
- Headings, columns, rows, and information with cells should be uncluttered and easy to read.
- Format information within cells consistently flush left or centered.
- When a table contains so many lines of information that it may be difficult to read or interpret, separate logical groups with extra spacing or alternative formatting (e.g., use double or boldface border lines).
- When several tables or figures appear in a document, assign each a figure number.

b. Page Placement.

- Center tables appearing within text. Exceptionally wide tables may extend to the margins.
- Center tables that appear alone on a page.

See section 1010, page 272, and figure 10.5 for information on using tables within text.

Use the Tables feature of your word processing program to help you make attractive tables quickly. Also, many word processing programs permit you to import spreadsheets into your documents to serve as tables, though you may have to adjust the table formatting once the spreadsheet has been inserted.

Title ODYSSEY ELECTRONICS

Subtitle Administrative Assistants

Employee Name	Social Security No.	Date of Birth	Date of Hire
M.J. Kimmeroth	379-90-7865	7-17-54	3-14-85
Maria Montez	286-30-7656	9-30-65	6-19-89
Lee Epstein	330-78-7642	3-15-68	8-17-90
Beatrice Windsor	345-90-8897	6-12-63	5-5-87

Column heads formatted consistently

Cell information formatted consistently

Fig. 10.19. Boxed table.

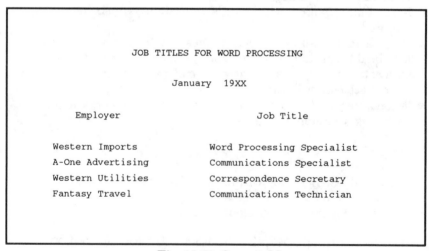

JOB TITLES FOR WORD PROCESSING

January 19XX

Employer	Job Title
Western Imports	Word Processing Specialist
A-One Advertising	Communications Specialist
Western Utilities	Correspondence Secretary
Fantasy Travel	Communications Technician

Fig. 10.20. Open table.

```
                    CIRCULATION SUMMARY

               Five Years Ending December 1993

Region    Manager         1991      1992      1993

North     J. Ryan        35,330    34,290    35,750
South     M. Peete       29,338    30,229    31,103
East      K. Wells       32,890    33,340    35,014
West      P. Kitts       36,110    36,895    36,451
```

Fig. 10.21. Ruled table.

NOTES

APPENDIXES
- Common DOS Commands
- Filing Rules
- Postal Service Guidelines
- Grammar and Language Terms
- Recommended Resources

APPENDIXES

NOTES

APPENDIX A

COMMON DOS COMMANDS

Below is a list of the most commonly used DOS commands. For more information on these and other DOS commands, see your DOS documentation or *MS/PC DOS Made Easy* by Edward J. Coburn (Paradigm, 1990).

BACKUP　　copies from the hard disk to a floppy disk; use the RESTORE command to copy the same files back from the floppy disk to the hard drive. Example *C:\LETTERS>BACKUP A:* backs up all files in LETTERS directory to disk in drive A.

CD　　CHANGE DIRECTORY. Example: *C:\MEMOS>CD\LETTERS* takes the user from the MEMOS directory to the LETTERS directory.

CHKDSK　　CHECK DISK; provides a status report of your disk. Example: *C:>CHKDSK B:* will check the status of the disk in the B drive, reporting on total memory used, total memory free, and any problems that exist on the disk.

COPY　　copies files between disks and directories. Example: *C:\LETTERS>COPY *.* A:* will copy all files from the LETTERS directory to the disk in drive A.

DATE　　changes the date stored in your computer. Example: *C:>DATE* displays the date and allows you to change or check it. The command TIME is used the same way to change or check the time stored in your computer.

DEL deletes files. Example: *C:\LETTERS>DEL *.** will delete all files from the LETTERS directory on the C drive. See *.*.

DIR DIRECTORY; lists files on a disk or in a specific directory. Example: *C:\LETTERS> DIR* will list all files in the LETTERS directory of drive C. *DIR |* will list the files one page at a time.

DISKCOPY copies everything, including formatting, from one disk to another. Example: *A:>DISKCOPY B:* will copy everything from the disk in drive A to the disk in drive B. The disk in drive B will be erased and reformatted (or simply formatted) before the copy process begins.

EDLIN EDIT LINE; allows you to edit single program lines within files and is often used for editing batch files. Example: *C:>EDLIN AUTOEXEC.BAT* will allow you to edit the AUTOEXEC.BAT file in your C drive.

EXE EXECUTE; not a DOS command but a standard file extension for files that execute (or start) a program. If you are not sure how to start a program, run a directory (see DIR) of the files in that program. The file using EXE as an extension is probably the file needed to start the program; therefore, at the prompt (>) type that filename and ENTER to start the program.

FORMAT	formats disks for information storage. Example: *C:>FORMAT A:* will format the disk in the A drive so it may be read and written to by the computer.
MD	MAKE DIRECTORY; creates a directory for information storage. Example: *C:>MD PRIVATE* will create a directory named PRIVATE on the C drive.
PROMPT	changes the form of the DOS prompt. Example: *C:>PROMPT What would you like?* will change the computer's prompt from *C:>* to *What would you like?* This command is often used in creating menus.
RD	REMOVE DIRECTORY; removes or deletes an empty directory. Example: *C: >RD LETTERS* deletes the LETTERS directory from the C drive. Files in this directory must be deleted (use the DEL command) before the RD command will work. Also, you must be in a directory other than the one you are removing.
RENAME	renames a file. Example: *C:>RENAME A:SMITH.LET SMYTH.LET* will rename the file SMITH.LET to SMYTH.LET.
RESTORE	used to copy back to the hard disk the files copied from the hard disk using the BACKUP command. See BACKUP.
TYPE	reveals a file's contents on the monitor. Example: *C:>TYPE AUTOEXEC.BAT* will put the AUTOEXEC.BAT file's contents on the screen for review or editing.
VER	VERSION; shows user which version of DOS is being used. Example: *C:>VER*

will reveal which version of DOS is being used.

.   a symbol that means ALL FILES. The asterisk (also known as a *wild card* symbol) can stand for any character or group of characters. Thus *.* stands for all filenames. Used with a command, *.* allows you to run an operation that affects all files. Example: *C:\LETTERS>COPY* *.*   *A:* will copy all files from the LETTERS directory on the C drive to the A drive. See DEL for another example.

APPENDIX B

FILING RULES

The Association of Records Managers and Administrators, Inc. (ARMA) recommends the standardized system of filing described in this appendix. The goal of the system summarized below is fast and easy retrieval of records based on consistent filing.

Basic Guidelines

1. Identify filing *units*. A *unit* is a number, a word, or a combination of numbers and words that make up the item (or *segment*) being filed:

Segment	*Units*
Patrick Hollings III	Patrick
	Hollings
	III

2. File by unit and then by letter or number within each unit:

Petersen, Robert	[e precedes o]
Peterson, Alice	[p precedes q]
Quincy, Elaine	

3. Consider each unit, including prepositions, articles (that is, *a, an, the*), and conjunctions; however, when *the* is the first unit, it becomes the last unit. Also, spell out symbols; for example, *e.g.* becomes *for example*, and *&* becomes *and*. Example:

Segment	*As Read and Filed*
A Night Out Restaurant	A Night Out Restaurant
The House of Lee	House of Lee The
Kipling & Jones Eatery	Kipling and Jones Eatery

4. File single-unit segments before multiple-unit segments. (This rule is known as "file nothing before something.") Example:

Pen and Leske Home and Garden

Penny Candy Housewares

Penny's Housewares Department

5. Ignore all punctuation marks. Consider hyphenated words a single unit:

Segment	*As Read and Filed*
Arnie's Plumbing	Arnies Plumbing
Hill-Phelps Plumbing	HillPhelps Plumbing
Remmie Plumbing, Inc.	Remmie Plumbing Inc

6. File Arabic (1, 2, 3, etc.) and Roman (i, ii, I, II, etc.) numerals sequentially before letters. Arabic numerals should precede Roman numerals:

Smith, William
Smith, William 3rd

Smith, William III
Smith, William Jr

7. Acronyms, abbreviations, and broadcasting call letters should be filed as single units. Example:

Segment	*As Read and Filed*
AFL-CIO	AFLCIO
S.A.D.D	SADD
WAXX Radio	WAXX Radio

8. Use the most common names or titles for filing. Cross-reference any other names or titles that might be used for filing requests. For example:

Monroe Marilyn

(See Baker Norma Jean)

Filing Personal Names

1. For simple names, use the last name (surname) followed by first name or initial, and the middle name or initial. When surnames have separate prefixes, consider the surnames and their prefixes a single unit:

Segment	*As Read and Filed*
Ian Mac Dougall	MacDougall Ian
Paul McCartney	McCartney Paul
Shannon O'Brien	OBrien Shannon
Winston O. Rand	Rand Winston O
Norma St. Louis	StLouis Norma
Brian Van Dam	VanDam Brian

2. Suffixes or titles accompany names to distinguish between identical last names. In that case, they are are filed as written, ignoring punctuation. Also, suffixes and titles are the last unit considered for filing:

Segment	As Read and Filed
James Jones Jr.	Jones James Jr
Jim Jones III	Jones Jim III
Governor Jim Jones	Jones Jim Governor
Major Jim Jones	Jones Jim Major
Mr. Jim Jones	Jones Jim Mr
Jim Jones, Ph.D.	Jones Jim PhD
Jimmy Jones	Jones Jimmy

3. File pseudonyms and royal or religious titles as they are written:

Segment	As Read and Filed
King Juan Carlos	King Juan Carlos
Madonna	Madonna
Pope John Paul	Pope John Paul
Prince Charles II	Prince Charles II
Sherlock Holmes	Sherlock Holmes
Sting	Sting

4. If foreign surnames are easily identifiable, file as you would any other name; however, if a surname and first name may be confused, file twice—by the last name and by the first name. Then refer to the complete name (last, first) in a cross reference:

Faljeno Moran
    (see Moran Faljeno)

Harper Joe

Moran Faljeno

Templeton Bonnie

Filing Organization Names

1. For business names, follow the basic guidelines above, filing the following segments in the order shown:

Segment	**As Read and Filed**
1-2-3 Go	123 Go
3M	3M
A-1 Laundry	A1 Laundry
AA	AA (See Alcoholics Anonymous)
The Birthday Party	Birthday Party The
Century 21	Century 21
Century Photo	Century Photo
I.B.M.	IBM
Mrs. Smith's Cookies	Mrs Smiths Cookies
St. Peter's Center	StPeters Center
WAXX Radio	WAXX Radio

Note: Names with numbers are filed before names with letters.

2. Consider place names and compass points in business names as their own units:

   Arkansas Light Company
   Brownsville Border Patrol
   East Chicago Development Center
   Northwest Bank

3. When filing government or political materials, use the governing body's name first, followed by the distinctive name of the department, office, and so on. Delete such phrases as *Office of* and *Department of.*

Federal Government:

Segment	As Read and Filed
United States Army	United States Government Army
United States Department of Housing and Urban Development	United States Government Housing and Urban Development
United States Department of the Treasury	United States Government Treasury

State and Local Governments:

Segment	As Read and Filed
Alsey County Department of Energy	Alsey County Energy
City of Inver Heights	Inver Heights
New York Department of Corrections	New York Corrections
Xavier County	Xavier County

4. When filing information from foreign countries and governments, use the distinctive name of the country:

Segment	As Read and Filed
Commonwealth of Australia	Australia
London, England	London England
The Netherlands	Netherlands The
South Africa	South Africa

For More Information

In addition to the more general guidelines above, ARMA offers suggestions for handling common filing problems. ARMA also recommends a procedure to follow when converting to or establishing an electronic filing system. For more information on these issues or on the general guidelines summarized above, contact ARMA at 4200 Somerset, Suite 215, Prairie Village, KS 66208.

APPENDIX C

POSTAL SERVICE GUIDELINES

The U.S. Postal Service has established the guidelines below to accommodate their automated processes, which involve electronic scanning of the information typed on envelopes. Following these guidelines will ensure that your mail is delivered quickly and accurately and will hold postage costs to a minimum. For further information on the following guidelines, contact your local post office.

Regular Mail

1. **Dimensions.** The physical size of the postcards and envelopes should fall within the following ranges:

   Postcards
Height	3 1/2" – 4 1/4"
Length	5" – 6"
Thickness	0.007" – 0.0095"

   Envelopes
Height	3 1/2" – 6 1/8"
Length	5" –11 1/2"
Thickness	0.009" –0.25"
	(must be flexible)

2. **Address Placement.** To be scanned fully, the address must be placed according to the guidelines below. See figure C.1 for illustrations of these guidelines:

   a. The entire address must fit into an imaginary rectangle whose bottom begins at 5/8" from the bottom of the envelope and whose top extends from 2 3/4" from the bottom of the envelope. The rectangle's sides are no less than 1" from either side of the envelope.

b. The area ⅝" from the bottom edge and 4-½" from the right side of the envelope must not be written in. The Postal Service will print a bar code in this area to facilitate the distribution process.

c. Any nonaddress information should be placed above the address because the scanner reads the address from bottom to top.

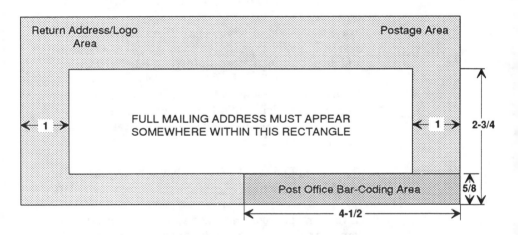

Figure C.1. Address placement on standard business envelope.

3. Address Contents and Appearance. See figure C.2 for examples of the guidelines given below:

a. Always type or machine-print your addresses if possible. Also, print with dark ink (preferably black) on a light background (preferably white).

b. Use all capital letters with no punctuation. (Note, however, that Postal Service scanners also can read addresses handwritten or keyed in the traditional uppercase and lowercase letter format, should your company prefer that style for regular business correspondence.) Use an extra space between words if you wish to set them off more than regular spacing suggests. Also, maintain an even left margin.

c. Use a type style in which characters do not touch or overlap. Avoid type styles such as italics or script, and do not use nonletter-quality dot matrix printing.

d. If envelopes have an address window, the address must be fully visible at all times through the window. A 1/8" to 1/4" clearance between address and window edge is preferred.

e. The bottom line of the address should be as parallel as possible to the bottom edge of the envelope, not slanted.

f. Always provide floor, suite, and apartment numbers and compass point information. (See examples in figure C.2.)

g. Use two-letter state abbreviations. *(See section 705, page 167.)* When abbreviating street addresses, use the standard abbreviations in figure C.3.

h. Use the ZIP+4 Code when possible. ZIP+4 Codes identify the region, city, neighborhood, and building of the addressee.

i. For international mailing, the name of the country of destination should stand alone on the bottom line, unless the destination is Canada, which uses a postal code.

Rural address

H E BROWN
RR 3 BOX 9
CANTON OH 44730-9521

Address with P.O. box

MR STANLEY DOE
LAST NATIONAL BANK
PO BOX 345
NEW YORK NY 10163-0345

Standard 3-line address

MR JAMES F JONES
4417 BROOKS ST NE
WASHINGTON DC 20019-4649

Address with building name and room number

ACME INSURANCE CO
CAREW TOWERS
300 E MAIN ST RM 1121
MEMPHIS TN 38166-1121

International addresses

MR THOMAS CLARK
17 RUSSEL DR
LONDON W1P 6HQ
ENGLAND

MS HELEN SANDERS
1010 CLEAR ST
OTTAWA ON K1A OB1
CANADA

Figure C.2. Sample address formats.

Courtesy Reply and Business Reply Mail

Guidelines for courtesy reply and business reply mail (postcards and envelopes) differ significantly from the guidelines for regular mail described above. When considering these business options, call your local postal service for guidelines. Once you have the guidelines, print a sample of the postcard or envelope you want to use, and ask your postal representative to review it before you print multiple copies.

Special U.S. Postal Services

Call your U.S. Postal Service for information on any of the following services:

- Insured, registered, and certified mail
- Return receipts
- Restricted and special delivery
- Special handling
- COD (collect-on-delivery) service
- Post office box and caller services
- Mailgram service
- Postage meter service
- Passport service
- ZIP and ZIP+4 Codes

Fast Mail Service

Overnight, second-day, and other fast mailing services are available through the U.S. Postal Service and through private couriers. The yellow pages of your local telephone book should list such services in your area.

Alley	ALY	Fork	FRK
Annex	ANX	Forks	FRKS
Arcade	ARC	Fort	FT
Avenue	AVE	Freeway	FWY.
Bayou	BYU	Gardens	GRNS
Beach	BCH	Gateway	GTWY
Bend	BND	Glen	GLN
Bluff	BLF	Green	GRN
Bottom	BTM	Grove	GRV
Boulevard	BLVD	Harbor	HBR
Branch	BR	Haven	HVN
Bridge	BRG	Heights	HTS
Brook	BRK	Highway	HWY
Burg	BG	Hill	HL
Bypass	BYP	Hills	HLS
Camp	CP	Hollow	HOLW
Canyon	CYN	Inlet	INLT
Cape	CPE	Island	IS
Causeway	CSWY	Islands	ISS
Center	CTR	Isle	ISLE
Circle	CIR	Junction	JCT
Cliffs	CLFS	Key	KY
Club	CLB	Knolls	KNLS
Corner	COR	Lake	LK
Corners	CORS	Lakes	LKS
Course	CRSE	Landing	LNDG
Court	CT	Lane	LN
Courts	CTS	Light	LGT
Cove	CV	Loaf	LF
Creek	CRK	Locks	LCKS
Crescent	CRES	Lodge	LDG
Crossing	Xing	Loop	LOOP
Dale	DL	Mall	MALL
Divide	DV	Manor	MNR
Dam	DM	Meadows	MDWS
Drive	DR	Mill	ML
Estates	EST	Mills	MLS
Expressway	EXPY	Mission	MSN
Extension	EXT	Mount	MT
Fall	FALL	Mountain	MTN
Falls	FLS	Neck	NCK
Ferry	FRY	Orchard	ORCH
Field	FLD	Oval	OVAL
Fields	FLDS	Park	PARK
Flats	FLT	Parkway	PKY
Ford	FRD	Pass	PASS
Forest	FRST	Path	PATH
Forge	FRG	Pike	PIKE

Figure C.3. Standard address abbreviations (U.S. Postal Service).

Pines	PNES
Place	PL
Plain	PLN
Plains	PLNS
Plaza	PLZ
Point	PT
Port	PRT
Prairie	PR
Radial	RADL
Ranch	RNCH
Rapids	RPDS
Rest	RST
Ridge	RDG
River	RIV
Road	RD
Row	ROW
Run	RUN
Shoal	SHL
Shoals	SHLS
Shore	SHR
Shores	SHRS
Spring	SPG
Springs	SPGS
Spur	SPUR
Square	SQ
Station	STA
Stravenue	STRA
Stream	STRM
Street	ST
Summitt	SMT
Terrace	TER
Trace	TRCE
Track	TRAK
Trail	TRL
Trailer	TRLR
Tunnel	TUNL
Turnpike	TPKE
Union	UN
Valley	VLY
Viaduct	VIA
View	VW
Village	VLG
Ville	VL
Vista	VIS
Walk	WALK
Way	WAY
Wells	WLS

Standard address abbreviations (continued).

APPENDIX D

GRAMMAR AND LANGUAGE TERMS

A summary of potentially difficult grammar and language terminology used in this manual is provided here:

Adjective—a word, phrase, or clause that modifies a noun or pronoun:

> A *long* report is due next week. [The word *long* modifies *report.*]

> The machine *running now* will shut off soon. [The phrase *running now* modifies *machine.*]

> The man *whose house I just sold* gave me a bonus. [The clause *whose house I just sold* modifies *man.*]

> See also *Modifier.*

Compound adjective—an adjective formed by combining two or more words:

> We made a *tax-free* purchase.

> Use an *up-to-date* dictionary.

Comparative adjective—the form of the adjective used when two things are compared:

> My raise was *higher* than your raise.

> My vacation was *more fun* than your   vacation.

Superlative adjective—the form of the adjective used when three or more things are compared:

My raise was the *highest*.

My vacation was the *most fun*.

Adverb—a word, phrase, or clause that modifies a verb, an adjective, or another adverb. Examples:

She had a *very* tired assistant. [The word *very* modifies the adjective *tired*.]

He keys *extremely* well. [The word *extremely* modifies the adverb *well*.]

She ran *to the conference room*. [The phrase *to the conference room* modifies the verb *ran*.]

When she left, I had to do it myself. [The clause *When she left* modifies the verb *had*.]

See also *Modifier*.

Comparative adverb—the form of the adverb used when two things are compared:

My assistant works *faster* than hers does.

My office runs *more smoothly* than his does.

Superlative adverb—the form of the adverb used when three or more things are compared:

My assistant works *fastest*.

My office runs most *smoothly*.

Appositive—word, phrase, or clause placed after a noun or noun phrase to explain it:

My favorite coworker, *Hilda,* invited me to lunch. [*Hilda is* a proper noun explaining the noun *coworker*; therefore, *Hilda* functions as an appositive.]

Mr. Dietrich, *my boss,* asked me to work late. [*My boss* identifies *Mr. Dietrich* and, therefore, functions as an appositive.]

See also *Adjective* and *Modifier.*

Clause—a group of words that functions as a unit in a sentence and contains both a subject and verb:

I can pick up lunch

when she comes in tomorrow

which I would love to see

as I see it

Dependent Clause—a clause that cannot stand alone as a sentence (sometimes called a subordinate clause):

when she comes in tomorrow

which I would love to see

as I see it

Introductory Clause—a dependent clause that comes before the main clause:

As I see it, she should be promoted soon.

Main Clause—a clause that can stand alone as a sentence (also called an independent clause):

She should be promoted soon.

Note: A sentence may have many clauses, but every sentence must have at least one main clause.

Comma Splice—a sentence error created by connecting (splicing) two main clauses with only a comma:

Wrong: Give me your office keys, I'll stop there and pick up those files.

Rewrite: Give me your office keys, and I'll stop there and pick up those files.

Complex Sentence—a sentence containing at least one independent clause and one or more dependent clauses:

I was not at home when the mail arrived.

Compound Sentence—a sentence consisting of two or more main clauses:

Give me your office keys, and I'll stop there and pick up those files.

She ate the sandwiches, I ate the salad, and Roger ate the pie.

Conjunction—a word or pair of words that connects words, phrases, or clauses:

I'd like *either* this *or* that. [Connects two words.]

He did come through *but* did not call us. [Connects two phrases.]

Give me your office keys, *and* I'll stop there and pick up those files. [Connects two clauses.]

I called *because* I couldn't find the information. [Connects two clauses.]

I called you yesterday; *however*, I found what I needed without your help. [Connects two clauses.]

Infinitive—a phrase consisting of the word *to* plus a verb; often introduces a longer phrase:

He said he wanted *to go.* [Simple infinitive phrase.]

He said he wanted *to go with us.* [Longer infinitive phrase.]

Modifier—any word, phrase, or clause that functions in a sentence as an adjective or adverb (see also *Adjective* and *Adverb*):

She wore a *blue* uniform. [Adjective]

They held the meeting *quickly.* [Adverb]

Bring me the file *kept on my desk.* [Adjective phrase]

Bring me the file *by the window.* [Adverb phrase]

That is the office *that I want.* [Adjective clause]

Essential modifier—a modifier whose purpose in the sentence is *to define* the thing it modifies and distinguish that thing from other things:

The story *that I heard* was that she would start on Monday. [The clause *that I heard* tells which *story* is being discussed and, therefore, defines *story.*]

Nonessential modifier—a modifier whose purpose is *to provide additional information* about the thing it modifies *without defining* that thing:

The story, *which I heard today*, is spreading around the office quickly. [The clause *which I heard today* adds information about *story* but does not tell which *story* and, therefore, does not define *story.*]

Noun—a word, phrase, or clause that names a person, place, thing, or idea and does not function as a modifier:

My *boss* asked *Fred* to read last year's department *report*.

Collective Noun—a noun that names a group:

family
staff
team
committee

Common Noun/Proper Noun—a common noun names a class or type of person, place, thing, or idea; a proper noun refers to and names a particular person, place, or thing:

Common Nouns	*Proper Nouns*
woman	Rhonda
manager	Ms. Wilson
building	Bentley Building
country	United States

Compound Noun—a noun formed by combining two or more words. Some are hyphenated, some are written as one word, and some are written as two words:

They sponsored a *sit-in*.

He managed the company's *database*.

Jean bought a *money order*.

Object—a word, phrase, or clause whose purpose in the sentence is to receive the action of the verb:

You must read the *report* carefully. [*Report* receives the action of the verb *read*—the report is being read.]

Participle—one of the three major forms of any verb; the form which, when used as a verb, is always used with a helping verb (usually *has, have,* or *had*). Often used (as a single word or a phrase) as an adjective also:

> We *have begun* already. [As verb.]

> *Begun on schedule,* the report was finished with time to spare. [As participial phrase modifying *report.*]

> *Beginning on schedule,* she hoped to finish with time to spare. [As participial phrase modifying *she.*]

Phrase—a group of words that functions as a unit in a sentence but does not contain both a subject and a verb:

> He ran *through the office door.*

> Roger, *a good friend and coworker,* called *to warn me.*

> *Running the copy machine* can be a challenge.

> *To work late* takes a lot of stamina.

Preposition—a word that begins a modifying phrase that shows a relationship between two parts of a sentence:

> He ran *through the office door.* [Phrase tells where *he ran;* preposition *through* relates *ran* to *door.*]

> The file cabinet *by the windows* is empty. [Phrase tells where the *cabinet* is; preposition *by* relates *cabinet* to *windows.*]

> The blackout lasts *until sunrise.* [Phrase tells how long the *blackout lasts;* preposition *until* relates *lasts* and *sunrise.*]

Give the money *to whoever will take it.* [Phrase
tells to whom *the money* should be given;
preposition *to* relates *the money* to *whoever will
take it.*]

Object of the Preposition—the noun or pronoun (or noun
phrase or clause) that ends a prepositional phrase; in
the examples above, *door, windows, sunrise,* and
whoever will take it.

Pronoun—a word that replaces and refers to a noun:

Bob said *he* could work for me tomorrow. [*He*
replaces *Bob* and refers to *Bob.*]

Reference (also **antecedent**)—the word the pronoun refers
to; in the example above, it is *Bob.*

Case—classification of pronouns:

1. Nominative—usually subject of sentence

He will work for me tomorrow.

2. Objective—usually object of sentence or object of
preposition

He avoided *me* and ran to *them.*

3. Possessive—shows ownership

Their office is on the highest floor.

4. Reflexive—ends with -self or -selves

We must trust *ourselves.*

Subject—a word, phrase, or clause that names the part of the
sentence responsible for the action of the verb:

This *office* gets on my nerves sometimes.

Running the copy machine can be a challenge.

Whoever thought of that deserves a raise.

Compound Subject—two or more subjects sharing the same verb:

Bob and *Roberta* are twins.

Transition— a conjunction or adverb (usually a word or phrase) that shows a connection between two ideas or a movement from one idea to the next:

I will go, *but* you must stay.

I invested foolishly and, *therefore*, lost my savings.

I should go somewhere exciting, *for example,* Hawaii or Mexico.

Next, let me tell you about our benefits.

Verb—a word or phrase that denotes action in a clause or, in the case of forms of the verb *be*, denotes the existence of something:

We *have begun* already.

If we *find* the mistake, we *should ask* Bill about it.

We *are* lucky.

Bigger profits *will come* soon.

Verb Tense—indicates time and time relationships:

Present Tense
She *wants* a raise.

Past Tense
She *wanted* a raise.

Perfect Tense
>
> She *has wanted* a raise. (Present perfect)
> She *had wanted* a raise. (Past perfect)
> She *will have wanted* a raise. (Future perfect)

Future Tense
>
> She *will want* a raise.

Verb Mood—indicates the manner in which the action is conceived:

Indicative Mood—makes a statement or asks a question:

> She *is* the corporate counsel.

> *Is* he the one who should receive the report?

Imperative Mood—gives a command or makes a request:

> *File* that letter with the others.

> Please *call* me about the conference.

Subjunctive Mood—expresses doubt, a wish, or a condition contrary to fact:

> I wish I *were* staff director.

> If I *were* you, I would attend the meeting.

APPENDIX E

RECOMMENDED RESOURCES

Well equipped workstations provide not only the tools workers need to do their jobs but also the necessary sources of information. Below is a summary of recommended resources:

Computer Program Documentation

Commercial software usually comes with its own documentation; however, you may find the documentation too difficult to use, or it may not be available at your workstation. If so, many guides to most popular software are available at bookstores or through publishers' catalogs. Preview these guides before buying them to ensure that you find the ones most helpful to you.

Dictionary

Many good choices exist. One of the best general-purpose dictionaries is the most recent edition of *Webster's New Collegiate Dictionary*. Be sure to use the most up-to-date dictonary available. In addition, several specialized dictionaries are available, including medical and biographical dictionaries.

Guide to Nonsexist Word Usage

A few of these guides are now commercially available. They offer practical suggestions for avoiding potentially offensive language. One option is Val Dumond's *The Elements of Non-sexist Usage: A Guide to Inclusive Spoken and Written English* (Prentice-Hall).

Parliamentary Procedure Guidelines

Use the most recent edition of *Robert's Rules of Order* to guide you in conducting formal meetings.

Spelling and Hyphenation Guide

Spelling and hyphenation guides are especially useful for those who do not write using a word processing system with a spelling checker. Such guides provide spellings for thousands of words and show how words should be divided at ends of lines, if necessary. One option is the most recent version of *The Word Book* (Houghton Mifflin).

Style Checker

For those who write on a computer, electronic style checkers are available. These checkers help writers identify not only possible errors but also weak and inappropriate writing. Two possibilities are the most recent versions of *Grammatik* (Reference Software International) or *RightWriter* (Que).

Style Manual

Style manuals provide guidelines for word usage, correct punctuation and capitalization, quoting borrowed material, acknowledging other sources of information, formatting, and page and document design. People who write research reports and produce company publications (e.g., newsletters, policy manuals, and annual reports) will find these manuals especially useful. Use *The Paradigm Reference Manual* for business correspondence, reporting, and most other business writing. The standard style manual for publishing is *The Chicago Manual of Style* (University of Chicago Press).

Telephone Book

Besides local telephone numbers, the introductory pages of your telephone book may offer information on:

- Various local and long-distance services available
- Services for people with special needs
- Repair services
- Information on telephone directory advertising
- Regulations dictating telephone use
- Area codes and time zones (sometimes ZIP Codes)
- Information on international calling

Thesaurus

Also called a *synonym finder,* a thesaurus is useful for helping business writers find the best word for any situation. Many word processing software packages have an on-line thesaurus. If your word processor does not, many good publications exist; any recent *Roget's* thesaurus should be thorough and easy to use.

ZIP Code Guide

Sources are available that list ZIP Codes for any city in the country. Two possibilities are the most recent editions of the *ZIP Code Finder* (Rand McNally & Co.) or the *ZIP Code Directory* (Arrow Publishing Co.). Your local post office will also have the ZIP Codes you need.

INDEX

Italics
  in business report, **306**
  to emphasize, **122**
  to indicate foreign words or phrases, **123**
  to indicate titles, **121-122, 300**
  to indicate words discussed as words, **122-123**
it's / its, **221**

J

Job titles, in inside address, **266**
justification, **242**
  in business letter formatting, **259-260**
  in interoffice memorandums, **281**
  in report formatting, **304**

K

K (or Kb), **243**

L

LAN, **243**
Language(s)
  capitalization of, **137-138**
  correcting sexist, **26-27, 47-50, 343**
  using positive, **25-26**
laptop computer, **243**
laser disk, **243**
laser printer, **243**
last / latest / past, **221**
latter / former, **218**
lay / lie, **221-222**
LCD, **243**
lead / led, **222**
Legal documents, numbers in, **157**
lend / loan / borrow, **211**
less / fewer, **217-218**
letter-quality printer, **243**
Letters

capitalization of, **138**
  periods after, in lists, **69-70**
  periods with, in outlines, **68-69**
lie / lay, **221-222**
light pen, **243**
like / as, **208-209**
Lists
  capitalization of first word in vertical, **131-132**
  colons to introduce, **98-101**
  using periods with items in, **70-71**
  using periods with letters and numbers in, **69-70**
literally, **223**
loan / lend / borrow, **211**
local area network (LAN), **243**
loose / lose, **223**

M

Main clause, **335**. *See also* Clause
  colon introducing the, **102**
  commas to separate phrases and dependent clauses after, **86**
mainframe computer, **244**
main memory, **244**
Margins
  in business letter formatting, **259**
  in interoffice memorandums, **281**
  in report formatting, **303-304**
may / can, **211**
Mb, **244**
Measurements
  abbreviations for units of, **172-174**
  numbers in, **150**
media / medium, **223**
memory, **244**
Memos. *See* Interoffice memorandums
menu, **244**
merge, **244**
Metric units, abbreviations of, **173**
micro-computer, **244**

modifying numbers, **156**
in money, **149**
in numbered objects, **149-150**
ordinal, **155-156**
in percentages, **151**
periods with, in outlines, **68-69**
with symbols and abbreviations, **152**
in time expressions, **147-148**
using periods after, in lists, **69-70**
and word division, **196**
words versus figures for expressing, **152-156**

O

Object(s), **138**
pronouns as, **52-53**
Objective case, **51**
for pronouns used as objects, **52-53**
Object of the preposition, **340**
Occupational titles, capitalization of, **141-142**
OCR, **245**
Official titles, capitalization of, **139-141**
offline, **245**
off of, **225**
off of / all of, **205**
online, **245**
on / onto, **219-220**, **225**
operating system, **245**
optical disk, **245**
or, **34**
to combine clauses, **87-89**
pronouns with more than one reference joined by, **49**
subject-verb agreement with, **34-35**
oral / verbal, **225**
or / and, **207**
Ordinal numbers, **155-156**
Organization
editing, **14**
of information, **4-5**
Organization names

abbreviations in, **166**, **267**
capitalization of official, **141**
filing, **323-325**
in inside address, **267**
Orphans, **260**
Outline
in business documents, **306**
alignment, **307**
division logic, **307**
parallel structure, **307**
section designations, **306-307**
capitalization of first words in sections, **132**
for first draft, **5**
periods with letters and numbers, **68-69**
spacing of, **69**
output, **245**

P

Paradigm Reference Manual, **344**
Paragraph
coherence in, **6, 7**
importance of strong, **6-7**
unity in, **6, 7**
Parallel structure
in business report, **307**
in paragraphs, **19**
parallel transmission, **245**
parent directory, **246**
Parentheses, **118**
to indicate nonessential sentence elements, **119-121**
to indicate nonessential sentences, **119**
with quotation marks, **115-116**
spacing with, **119**
Parliamentary procedure guidelines, **344**
Participle, **339**
passed / past, **225**
Passive voice, **8-9**
past / last / latest, **221**
Past perfect tense, **41**
Past tense, **341**
peace / piece, **226**

NOTES

NOTES